The Wisteria Hysteria

By Daphne C. Murrell

NOTICE

The amateur and stock acting rights to this work are controlled exclusively by MOUNTAIN PARADISE PUBLISHERS and DAPHNE C. MURRELL without whose permission in writing no performance of it may be given. Royalty fees are given by personal contact through correspondence.

All inquiries concerning amateur and stock rights should be addressed to:

MOUNTAIN PARADISE PUBLISHERS
1911 4th Street SE
Red Bay, Alabama 35582
or
slappydaph@att.net

Copyright © 2014 by Mountain Paradise Publishers

All rights reserved.

ISBN-13: 978-0692253441 (Mountain Paradise Publishers)
ISBN-10: 0692253440

DEDICATION

This play is dedicated to the BTCPA,
the Bay Tree Council for the Performing Arts,
in Red Bay, Alabama—proof that big entertainment can
most certainly come in small packages. While communities
are choosing to delete the arts, especially in our schools,
Red Bay has kept it alive through theater.
Bravo!

Photos by Scotty Kennedy

ORIGINAL CAST

(Bottom, left to right) TAMI-TINA: Mary Elizabeth Moore; NILANSA: Hannah Jackson; SUSIE: Georgia Jeffreys; LOUISA: Tina Smith; FANCY: Heather Mitchell Lanham; TINA-TAMI: Charis Murrell

(Top, left to right) GRANDMA KAT: Mary Dyer; ARMANDO: Rhett Jackson; BILLY: River Dolan; BUTLER: Richard Twilley; RANDOLPH: Scotty Kennedy; BENTLEY: Jerry Self; MAID: Abbey Jones

The Wisteria Parlor

The Bedroom

Charades in Bedroom

Table of Contents

ACT ONE	Scene One	1
ACT ONE	Scene Two	11
ACT ONE	Scene Three	33
ACT TWO	Scene One	44
ACT TWO	Scene Two	67

Cast of Characters

Billy Cavanaugh	*Accountant*
Susie Smith	*Billy's Fiance'*
Randolph Cavanaugh	*Billy's Father*
Louisa Cavanaugh	*Billy's Mother*
Butler	*Announces All Who Enter Wisteria*
Nilansa Cavanaugh	*Actress/Randolph's Sister*
Tami-Tina Cavanaugh	*Twin Actress/Nilansa's Daughter*
Tina-Tami Cavanaugh	*The Other Twin*
Grandma Kat	*Randolph's Mother*
Maid	*Grandma's Caretaker*
Bentley Cavanaugh	*Actor/Randolph's Brother*
Fancy Cavanaugh	*Country Singer/Randolph's Sister*
Armando	*The Pool Guy*

ACT ONE
Scene One

SCENE: *Billy Cavanaugh is standing in front of the curtain at a park with an open ring box in his hand. A bench is over to one side of the stage.*

BILLY: I can do this. I can propose ... again. I know she's rejected me twice, but not because she doesn't love me—I have to remember that. She doesn't want to marry me unless she can meet my family first. *(sighs as he closes the ring box)* If she only understood what she was asking! This could be really devastating ... or really great. What if she says "yes" this time? It could happen! She could have finally decided that I'm enough ... maybe—that she doesn't have to see "the tributaries from which I've flowed." *(shakes his head)* Or this could be Round Three of the whole thing over again. So what do I do if she says no and insists on meeting the family? Do I do it? Do I take her to Wisteria? And what about ... them? What will they do? How will they act?

SUSIE: *(from offstage)* Billy! Are you here?

BILLY: *(beginning to panic)* Oh no! Already? *(fumbles to put ring box in his pocket)* Deep breaths ... I can do this. I can. *(tries to collect his composure)*

SUSIE: *(she enters with a bright, spring hat and dress)* There's my handsome man! *(they take hands and she kisses his cheek)* Hope I didn't keep you waiting too long.

BILLY: For you never? *(drop hands)*

SUSIE: Things were crazy at the bank today. Old Mr. Wallace came in just as the manager said gold was up again. Mr. Wallace thought he said it was a hold-up. The poor, old thing dropped to the floor and started yelling, "Don't shoot! Don't shoot! I ain't even been to the teller yet! I ain't got no money!" It took us ten minutes to convince him there was no robbery ... and twenty minutes to get him on his feet again.

BILLY: *(preoccupied and nervous)* That's nice.

SUSIE: It is?

BILLY: I was thinking *(takes her hand and leads her to the bench)*, why don't you sit here *(helps her sit)* and I'll stand here.

SUSIE: Okay.

BILLY: *(looks over the situation and shakes his head)* No, that's not right. You stand *(helps her stand)* and I'll sit. *(embarrassed)* No! That's definitely not right! *(jumps up)*

SUSIE: Billy, what's wrong? Why are you so jumpy?

BILLY: I just want everything to be perfect.

SUSIE: It's a beautiful day—the weather is just right, the birds are singing, there's a brisk little breeze. I'd say mission accomplished. It is perfect!

BILLY: Good. I'm glad you think so. See, there are some things we really need to discuss. I've put them off too long.

SUSIE: Is this about my taxes again? *(plops down on bench)* I'm so sorry, Billy. That fact that you're an accountant magnifies my biggest flaw—keeping up with receipts. I've tried to remember about that little box you gave me, but ...

BILLY: No, no, no. It's nothing like that.

SUSIE: Okay ... there's something else about me that you're having trouble with?

BILLY: Well, yes. *(he sits next to her and takes her hand)* We've been seeing each other for three years now.

SUSIE: Three wonderful years.

BILLY: Right. That's my point. Life with you is wonderful—completely wonderful.

SUSIE: Why, thank you, Mr. Cavanaugh. I'm glad you think so.

BILLY: So, I keep hoping … praying … dreaming … *(he slips from the bench to one knee and fumbles in his pocket for the ring box)*

SUSIE: *(sadly)* Oh, Billy, no … don't tell me you're gonna propose again. *(she get up)*

BILLY: Susie, don't. Look, I don't know what else to do. I love you—you love me. We spend all our time together. It doesn't make sense.

SUSIE: *(she starts to walk away)* I've told you my conditions for marriage, Billy! I can't imagine walking down the aisle with someone never having met his family! I want to know *(he mouths these words with her)* the tributaries from which you've flowed! I don't want there to be any secrets between us!

BILLY: This is the only one!

SUSIE: Yes! And it's a big one! A really big one! I don't have a clue about your family! What am I supposed to think about this intelligent, handsome, accomplished young man when he refuses to share his past with me? Your past is a part of who you are. I can't pretend it didn't exist.

BILLY: But you don't understand! My family's not … normal.

SUSIE: So what exactly does that mean? Does your mama have a beard? Was your daddy raised by wolves? Are they circus people?

BILLY: No! They're not that kind of weird! Why would you come up with something like that?

SUSIE: *(dropping her jaw in shock)* Because sometimes when it's late at night and I'm lying alone in my bed and I can't sleep ... because I'm still alone even though the man of my dreams has proposed twice ...

BILLY: ... three times now ...

SUSIE: Exactly! And I lie there and wonder what could be so bizarre about his family that he would be willing to deny us wedded bliss over them! Pardon me for letting my tired, worn-out imagination run a little wild.

BILLY: You don't understand.

SUSIE: Enlighten me ... please! I'm beginning to think that maybe you're embarrassed about me!

BILLY: Never!

SUSIE: Well, I don't want to think that, but nothing else makes sense.

BILLY: I have no idea what ... how ... I don't know what they'd do to you.

SUSIE: *(looks utterly shocked)* What? Are they ... convicted felons or something? Are they on the run? In the witness protection program?

BILLY: Susie ...

SUSIE: Do you think they would murder me or ...

BILLY: No!

SUSIE: Then what, Billy!? What!? What could be so horrendous that you would be willing to sacrifice our love over it? It's not right, Billy! It's not right ... and it's not ... fair. *(she starts to leave)*

BILLY: *(going after her)* No! Please don't go! Wait!

SUSIE: I'm tired of this. I just am. *(leaving)*

BILLY: *(desperate)* Okay! *(she turns)* I'll ... tell you.

SUSIE: *(hopeful)* Really? The whole ugly truth? Holding nothing back?

BILLY: *(nodding)* The whole ugly truth.
(He trudges slowly to the bench and she follows. They sit.)

SUSIE: *(taking his hand)* I want to assure you that whatever you tell me, I promise I won't think any differently of you.

BILLY: Don't be so sure. *(long pause as he gathers his courage)* Are you familiar with Randolph Demetrius Cavanaugh? Louisa Henrietta Cavanaugh?

SUSIE: Of course. I used to watch their show every Saturday night on TV. And I love all their movies, especially the one when ... *(the truth begins to dawn)* ... Wait. Are you telling me you're related somehow to Randolph Demetrius and Louisa Henrietta ... Cavanaugh? *(he nods slowly)* Oh ... my ... gosh ...

BILLY: My parents.

SUSIE: Is this a joke? Are you toying with me now?

BILLY: They're my parents. I'm their only child.

SUSIE: Then that means you're ... you're ... little William Desmond Cavanaugh? *(he nods)* You used to come out with them whenever they sang the last song on each show! I always wondered what happened to him ... you. I didn't recognize you without the ... head gear ... and the ... leg braces.

BILLY: *(he sighs in embarrassment)* Well, I do have perfect teeth now and am no longer bow-legged or pigeon-toed.

SUSIE: Wow ... I mean ... wow. *(pause)* Why did you want to keep this from me? Are you embarrassed about the ... braces or something?

BILLY: *(he stands)* This is where it gets hard.

SUSIE: I really don't understand.

BILLY: When I was in college, everyone knew who I was.

SUSIE: *(still is shock)* I can imagine. Your parents are probably the biggest movie stars of their time. I've literally seen every movie they've made ... watched reruns of all their shows.

BILLY: That complicated my ... romantic life considerably.

5

SUSIE: In what way?

BILLY: Every wanna-be actress in that college fell head over heels in love with me.

SUSIE: Well, you are a cutie. A little on the geeky-nerdy side, but I find that completely adorable.

BILLY: They all acted like they did too. I was the only Cavanaugh that stayed out of show business. I was the only one who went to college. These girls would latch on to me like white on rice and then plead with me to take them to Wisteria.

SUSIE: *(nodding)* The Cavanaugh Mansion.

BILLY: Once we were there, I was the last thing on their minds. I didn't even exist. I was an inconvenience and merely a means to their end ... which happened to be somehow impressing my family so much they would be given an immediate career in show business.

SUSIE: *(standing and going to him)* Oh, Billy, I'm so sorry.

BILLY: It was quite humiliating ... for me ... for my family. The last girl I took actually made a play for my Uncle Bentley.

SUSIE: Bentley Magnum Cavanaugh? He's your uncle? The action hero, movie star and producer, Hunk of the Year Award four years in a row?

BILLY: Yep.

SUSIE: It's hard to believe you two are related. He's so *(searching carefully for a word)* ... outgoing.

BILLY: I was so gullible that it was plain humiliating. My family, all of them, said I'd better never bring another girl home again.

SUSIE: Billy, it wasn't your fault. You're a good-hearted man ... you're a responsible and ... you're a sweet, gentle man.

BILLY: Every girl swore to me she was different than the last. *(sighs)* They were very good actresses, Susie, very good.

SUSIE: Is that why it took so long for you to ask me out on a legitimate date?

BILLY: Sort of. I was gun shy. I had given up in college. Everybody knew who I was, who my parents were, the family I belonged to. It was pointless. I just holed myself up in my room, walled my life off, and went as far away from Wisteria and Hollywood as I possibly could when I graduated.

SUSIE: Well, I can guarantee you this—there's not a person in Blue Bay, Alabama that suspects your true identity at all. *(something suddenly occurs to her)* Billy, you fit in so well down here, but you're not from the South? How did you manage that?

BILLY: If Fancy Cavanaugh can get away with it, so can I.

SUSIE: Oh, my gosh! Oh, my gosh! *(fans herself with excitement)* Fancy Tansy Cavanaugh? She's my favorite country singer ever! I tried to get a ticket to her Broadway show, ***Annie's Got A Rifle***, when I was in New York, but it was sold out the week I was there. I bought the DVD last Christmas. It was my favorite gift to myself.

BILLY: Gee—wish I had known. I could have gotten a signed copy. Would have cost a lot less than that diamond necklace I got you.

SUSIE: *(almost sadly)* You do realize now that I know, you have to take me ... you have to prove to them that I really love you.

BILLY: We don't have to go. Let's just pretend they don't exist.

SUSIE: No. I have to meet them ... I have to show them I adore YOU ...not THEM.

BILLY: They'll all be there, you know ... glaring at you, testing you.

SUSIE: Is Katherine Jeanine Cavanaugh still alive?

BILLY: Oh, yeah. She's the scariest of them all.

SUSIE: Billy! How can you say that? She's a sweet little old lady!

BILLY: Grandma Kat? Her mind's totally gone. She's sort of stuck in this audition mode for **Gone With the Wind**.

SUSIE: She should have beat Vivian Leigh for the role of Scarlett.

BILLY: Yeah, that's what she thinks too. And she's a little unpredictable nowadays. Since Grandpa Linus's death, she just seems lost.

SUSIE: *(another thought of excitement occurs)* Oh, my gosh, Billy! Will Nilansa be there? Nilansa Elizabeth Cavanaugh?

BILLY: Dad's sister ... chances are high.

SUSIE: She has to be the most glamorous movie star ever! *(looks at her clothes)* I'm gonna have to go shopping! There's no way I can face ... Nilansa ... looking so ...plain.

BILLY: You do realize she's aged considerably since her last movie? You could out-glamour her easily in just sweat pants and a t–shirt.

SUSIE: Billy! Don't be so mean! She has sacrificed her career to raise her two girls! *(another scream)* The twins! Will the twins be there? *(he nods)* Ahhhh! No way! No way! They have got be the most adorable girls I've ever seen!

BILLY: Really?

SUSIE: Have you never seen their show?

BILLY: TV? No—real life with them is more than enough. To actually *force* myself to watch them would be a form of psychological torture.

SUSIE: How can you say that? They're as cute as can be!

BILLY: Susie, life doesn't always imitate art.

SUSIE: I am just shocked ... purely shocked. Will I really get to meet them all?

BILLY: They all live there on and off ... all the Cavanaughs ... except me. *(he sighs)*

SUSIE: *(shakes her head)* I had no idea ... really ... no idea at all that you came from that kind of background. Never in a million years ... seriously.
BILLY: You need to understand that you're going there with 2 ½ strikes against you already.
SUSIE: But there's one big difference. *(she puts her arms around him and pulls him close)* I happen to be madly in love with William Desmond Cavanaugh ... and have no desire whatsoever to become a ... *star*.
BILLY: No, you're not in love with William Desmond— you're in love with plain ol' Billy Cavanaugh, accountant, a man who punches a calculator all day long and thinks it's the second greatest thing in life.
SUSIE: Second greatest? What would be the first?
BILLY: Hasn't happened yet. The day you agree to be my wife will be the greatest day of my life.
SUSIE: Oh, Billy. *(she kisses him)*

BLACKOUT

ACT ONE
Scene Two

SCENE: *In the formal living area of Wisteria Mansion. There is a stairway leading up to the main entrance in the back center of the room. Off to the right is a couch in front of a shelf full of awards. To the left are a couple of formal chairs with a wet bar standing behind them. Randolph is sitting on the couch and reading a script while the butler stands at his post at the top of the stairs. Louisa enters.)*

LOUISA: Are they here yet, Randolph?
RANDOLPH: Have you heard them announced?
LOUISA: I was out by the pool. Armando's got some kind of machine going out there. I couldn't hear myself think I if I wanted to.
RANDOLPH: It's too early anyway. He's not due for another thirty minutes.
LOUISA: This is William, dear. The boy would be early for a root canal.
RANDOLPH: *(preoccupied with his reading)* True.
LOUISA: What are you perusing there? *(looking over his shoulder)*
RANDOLPH: A script actually.
LOUISA: *(surprised)* Seriously? You're really considering taking on a project?
RANDOLPH: Perhaps.
LOUISA: What is it?

RANDOLPH: An interesting little period piece from an independent film maker.

LOUISA: Independent? Sounds horrid.

RANDOLPH: Not at all. It's quite the rage now.

LOUISA: What's the title? If it has a good title, that's half the draw. *(goes to wet bar and pours herself a drink)*

RANDOLPH: ***Irish Mutiny***.

LOUISA: Hmmm ... I'll have to think on that one a bit.

RANDOLPH: What did he say was the name of this girl? Sally, Sandy, Slappy?

LOUISA: Susie.

RANDOLPH: Susie ... not a very ... intriguing name, is it?

LOUISA: I'm trying not to think about her. I'm just glad we'll see William again. His visits have become so infrequent since he graduated from that college.

RANDOLPH: Imagine—a Cavanaugh graduating from college.

LOUISA: Imagine a Cavanaugh needing a reason to graduate from college.

RANDOLPH: True. *(stands and goes center)* When you consider the doors of show business have always swung wide open for us, it's hard to imagine why one would choose to strain one's brain in such a manner.

LOUISA: I don't think William's brain is wired quite the same as the rest of the Cavanaughs. However, he has a heart of gold. *(raises her glass)*

RANDOLPH: And a legacy of gold *(motions toward awards)* ... which every girl he has ever dated has tried to tap into. I'm trying hard to hope that this Slippy will be different.

LOUISA: Susie, dear. Her name is Susie. *(joins Randolph in center)*

RANDOLPH: Susie, Sassy, whatever—let's just hope we can scare her away before her greedy little hands implant themselves too deeply in his pockets ... or our pockets.

LOUISA: Agreed. If we can manage to pry this little Susie away, I'll feel much better. He's too kind-hearted for his own good, Randolph—and frankly, he's just too gullible.

RANDOLPH: Agreed, but at some point he will have to stand up for himself— *(goes to shelf and straightens awards)*

LOUISA: —and hopefully at some point he will find a true soul mate.

BUTLER: I believe Mr. William and his lady friend have arrived.

LOUISA: Oh, dear. *(places down her glass and nervously joins Randolph)*

RANDOLPH: Stiff upper lip, sweetie. She won't be around for long. Remember—the whole family will be arriving shortly. Once you get them all together and the skeletons start eeking out of the closets, it's enough to drive anyone insane ... even a Cavanaugh.

LOUISA: I hope you're right.

(Susie and William appear at the top of the stairs with William carrying their luggage.)

BUTLER: Hear ye! Hear ye, one and all! Now presenting Master William Desmond Cavanaugh, the counter, and his lady friend ... Miss *(he pauses with uncertainty and Susie whispers her name to him)* Susie Smith. Really?

BILLY: *(as he goes downstairs)* I'm not a counter—I'm an accountant.

(At this point, Louisa and Randolph step into roles and play everything overly dramatic.)

LOUISA: Dear William, sweet son of my loins!

RANDOLPH: I believe the loins would be mine, dear. He's the son of your womb.

LOUISA: Dear William, sweet son of my womb!

BILLY: Hello, Mother. Interesting greeting.

LOUISA: How marvelous to see you again! *(formally hugs Billy)* It has been too, too long! My heart nearly breaks, precious. You do know that, don't you?

BILLY: Sorry about that. *(sets luggage down at bottom of stairs)* It's hard to get away from the office. I stay pretty busy most of the time.

RANDOLPH: *(awkwardly shakes Billy's hand)* Yes, I suppose so, with that counting business. I've never fully understood that. Why would you count for a living? What exactly do you count anyway?

BILLY: Not "counting," Father, "accounting." I'm an accountant.

RANDOLPH: Okay … I guess I'm an a-actor then. Whatever, just glad to see you back here at Wisteria again.

(Susie clears her throat.)

BILLY: How rude of me. I'm so sorry. *(takes Susie's hand)* Mother, Father, this is the amazing woman I'm going to marry—Susie Smith.

SUSIE: I'm so honored to meet you both! I have loved your work for as long as I can remember!

LOUISA: What a sweet dear you are! *(gives her a formal hug on both sides of the face)* I can tell our William has certainly picked a prize apple among the bushel here.

SUSIE: Oh, my, what a sweet thing to say.

LOUISA: It was, wasn't it?

RANDOLPH: Yes, dear, quite. *(Louisa makes him shake Susie's hand)* Did you make that up off the cuff, or was it a line from one of your films?

LOUISA: I believe it was completely ad-libbed.

RANDOLPH: *(clapping)* Bravo!

BILLY: Anyway, we wanted to visit with you a bit and let you all have the chance to get to know each other.

LOUISA: Did my ears deceive me, or did you say that you were already planning to marry?

BILLY: Yes, Mother. We're planning a quiet little ceremony back in Alabama in two months.

LOUISA: I'm sure all *that* will change after your visit here.

RANDOLPH: *(quickly steps between Susie and Louisa)* What she means is that once Sally has visited Wisteria, she will surely want the wedding here!

LOUISA: But, of course! It's so comforting to know that you've managed to find happiness ... out there ... somewhere.

RANDOLPH: And what is it that you do, Sassy?

BILLY: Susie!

RANDOLPH: Susie, yes ... what is it that you do, Susie?

SUSIE: I'm a teller.

LOUISE: *(excited)* How marvelous! Great Uncle Barnabas Hampton Cavanaugh was a teller, as you call it, in the theaters of old. Back then they referred to it as a "narrator."

RANDOLPH: *(slapping Billy on the back)* Good job, old boy ... finding a girl in the business!

LOUISE: Who would have thought that?

SUSIE: *(trying to explain the mistake)* Oh, no ... you see, I'm not a ...

RANDOLPH: So, you've decided to give the old ball and chain a try? *(moves to bar for a drink. Billy follows and sits in chair. Ladies go to couch and sit. Once Randolph has drink, he sits in other chair.)*

BILLY: Yes, sir. I can't imagine trying to live the rest of my life without Susie by my side.

LOUISA: What a sweet, sweet thought.

SUSIE: I hope our marriage will be as lasting and fulfilling as yours has been. There aren't many in show business who seem to pull that off.

LOUISA: *(laughing)* Oh, my ... the Cavanaughs alone could present a who's who of failed marriages in the business! Are you familiar with Nilansa Elizabeth?

SUSIE: Yes, ma'am. I've seen all ...

LOUISA: Five marriages! Five! All actors too! You would think at some point she would just give up! Then poor Fancy—she fell head over heels for that cad, Bobby Bill McDill, when they were touring together. You would have thought she had a little more sense in picking a husband. We all knew it would never last.

SUSIE: I remember all the news surrounding the divorce. Bobby Bill was ruthless.

LOUISA: *(goes back to bar for her drink)* You have no idea, sweet girl, how ruthless he really was. Fancy finally hid out here at Wisteria for months just to avoid the press. And then there's Bentley. Heavens, for such a handsome man you would think he could find someone to settle down with.

SUSIE: Does he really have ... flings ... with all his leading ladies?

LOUISA: *(looking around as if she should make sure no one hears)* You would not believe the parade of women he has brought back here ... some even married. If only he could be as level headed as dear William and find a sweet narrator like you to settle down with.

SUSIE: Oh, no, ma'am, I'm not a narrator—I'm a teller.

LOUISA: I'm sorry, dear. I'm afraid I'm guilty of falling back to the old phrases and labels at times. As Grandpa Linus used to say, "I'm just an old dog digging up my old, comfortable bones."

(At this point, and every time Grandpa Linus is quoted, everyone except Susie always makes an "L" with the thumb and forefinger, kisses it, points to heaven, then drags it over the heart saying, "May he rest in peace.")

RANDOLPH: Somehow I don't envision Bentley being taken with someone like Slappy here.

BILLY: Father, her name is Susie!

RANDOLPH: Oh, that's right. Anyway, Bentley and William were so different. After a day of playing together Bentley would always come in so frustrated. He claimed William had no imagination whatsoever.

BILLY: *(gets up and acts out this description)* He used to tie me up, gag me and blindfold me, then threaten to drag me behind his bike if I didn't obey his every command. He'd make me dress like a girl, lie across the railroad tracks on the other side of the fence and scream, "Save me, Bentley!"

LOUISA: What fun!

RANDOLPH: The boy always did have a flair for the dramatic. Pure acting was in his blood. He reeked of it!

LOUISA: *(sadly)* It was his desire ... his calling ... his destiny.

RANDOLPH: Alas ... *(Randolph and Louisa click their glasses and drink in Bentley's honor)*

SUSIE: *(goes to stand by Billy)* He's very good. I've seen all his movies.

LOUISA: *(suspiciously)* Have you now? You sweet, dear girl ... supporting the arts like you do. Have you really seen all of his films.

SUSIE: Oh, yes ... in fact I've seen all your films too, Miss Louisa, Mr. Randolph. I loved your television show.

LOUISA: You are a prized gem among a vessel of lifeless rocks.

RANDOLPH: Oh, yes! Very good, dear! A prized gem.

SUSIE: I couldn't believe it when Billy finally told me who you were. I've even seen all the reruns from when he was little. I couldn't believe my Billy was little William Desmond!

(Billy is trying to keep her from saying anymore and is motioning her to be quiet.)

LOUISA: Imagine someone so young being familiar with our work, Randolph.

RANDOLPH: Indeed! It's hard to believe you would have seen our old-timer shows.

LOUISA: It's been so long since we've done anything.

SUSIE: You two were classic stars. You really should never have retired.
(Billy nervously tries to drag her away from the conversation)
RANDOLPH: I have been considering taking a more mature role of late ... something with meat to it that I can sort of sink my thespian teeth into.
SUSIE: Oh, that would be wonderful! What is it?
RANDOLPH: **Irish Mutiny**. It requires an accent, however.
LOUISA: Oh, dear, darling, you have always struggled with accents. Why would you even consider such a role? "Stick with what you know," as Grandpa Linus always said.
(All but Susie do Linus salute)
RANDOLPH: *(Suddenly an idea hits him. He puts down his glass and grabs the script.)* Why not run these lines with me a moment, Louisa, and let Sally here be the judge of my accent?
BILLY: Susie!
RANDOLPH: So sorry. I've always had trouble remembering names. *(hands the script to Louisa and she puts down her glass)* Start at the top of page 45, will you?
(Susie excitedly drags Billy to the couch where they sit as she eagerly awaits the performance.)
LOUISA: Very well, if you insist. *(she reads very dramatically)* "Charles! Whatever has happened to your arm?"
RANDOLPH: *(in an Irish brogue acting out the scene bigger than life)* "Alas, mi dear, but a gigantic creature with rows of razor sharp teeth plunged itself into the vessel! I alone faced it ... eye to eye ... darin' it to come any nearer! I reached out me hand, shoved it back off the ship, but just as it was about to sink beneath the surface, it opened it's blazin' mouth and bit me arm right off!"
LOUISA: *(clapping as Susie cheers with her)* Bravo! Bravo! That was unspeakably marvelous, dear! I can tell you've put some work into this.

RANDOLPH: Oh, not really. Just read through it a few times. *(grabs script back)*

BILLY: Funny, your memory seemed fine just then.

*(Nilansa and twins appear at top of stairs.
As they are announced they walk down the stairs.
Everyone stands as they enter.)*

BUTLER: Hear ye! Hear ye, one and all! Presenting Miss Nilansa Elizabeth Cavanaugh, Emmy winning, Tony winning, Oscar winning actress and singer of both stage and screen, and her two brilliantly talented twin daughters, Miss Tami-Tina Yolanda Cavanaugh, and Miss Tina-Tami Miranda Cavanaugh, stars of the hit television series, "Who's Your Sister?"

RANDOLPH: Dearest sister and delightful nieces! My, how you've all grown since I last saw you.

NILANSA: How we've *all* grown, Randolph? *(formal hugs)* Surely you're not calling me "old." That would be a bit hypocritical, wouldn't it, brother dear?

RANDOLPH: Now, now, Nilansa, we all age. The key is to remember what Grandpa Linus used to say—"You're only as old as the greasepaint makes you look."

*(All but Susie do Linus salute.
Randolph goes back to his chair for his glass and script
and begins reading again)*

LOUISA: *(to the twins)* And look at these precious dears! I believe you two become more darling with each passing day.

TAMI-TINA: Why, thank you, Aunt Louisa! You are so sweet to say that. *(hugs)*

TINA-TAMI: Right ... sweet. *(leans away from Louis's hug)*

LOUISA: And Nilansa, dear. *(very strained greeting)* I suppose you have movie offers coming in right and left these days.

NILANSA: Oh, my, Louisa, just as many as you do, I'm sure. However, I do spend most of my time managing the budding careers of my two daughters ... award-winning actresses ... committed to the business. You can't even imagine how fulfilling it is to have your children follow so successfully in your footsteps. *(immediately to Billy)* Oh, dear William! *(greets him)* How wonderful to see you again! And what is it that you're doing these days?

BILLY: I'm an accountant, Aunt Nilansa.

NILANSA: Oh, yes! *(bitingly)* You must be so proud, Louisa.

LOUISA: Well, he was always quite the independent thinker. Fortunately for me that meant I had to focus on honing my own skills rather than following my child around shmoozing with producers hoping to rekindle a snuffed out career.

NILANSA: *(sneering)* Why, you pretentious old ... *(gaining control)* I'm sorry—was there actually some project *you* had picked up recently? Are you working again ... for the first time in, oh let's see, how many years?

LOUISA: Come, dears. *(motions twins to follow her to couch)* Are you familiar with the twins, Susie? Have you ever seen their show?

SUSIE: Oh, yes ma'am. Who hasn't? *(to the twins)* I love all those pranks you play as twin sisters on the show. It must be fun being identical twins.

TAMI-TINA: You have no idea! People get us confused all the time. It's almost like we're the same person! We even finish each other's ... *(Tina-Tami isn't paying attention, so Tami-Tina elbows her)* ... we finish each other's ...

TINA-TAMI: Oh ... sentences ... yeah ... right. We do that ... sometimes. *(goes to chair and plops)*

SUSIE: Cute. *(extends her hand eagerly to Nilansa))* And Miss Nilansa, I am so honored to meet you. You've always been one of my favorite actresses.

NILANSA: *(hesitantly and formally takes Susie's hand with a single shake)* So, you are Billy's latest girlfriend?
BILLY: Fiancé', Aunt Nilansa. This is Susie.
NILANSA: Going to be one of the family now, hey?
SUSIE: I sure hope to.
(Grandma Katherine enters from downstairs. The Butler quickly runs to her side to announce her.)
BUTLER: Hear ye! Hear ye, one and all! Presenting the honorable Miss Katherine Jeanine Cavanaugh, award-winning actress of the ...
GRANDMA: *(grabs the butler by the collar)* Rhett Butler! I love you!
BILLY: Grandma! *(helps release the butler who runs back to his spot up the stairs)* It's me—William Desmond.
GRANDMA: Charmed, I'm sure.
BILLY: I want you to meet my wife-to-be. *(motions Susie over)* Grandma, this is Susie Smith. And Susie, this is my sweet Grandma Kat.
SUSIE: You have no idea how honored I am.
GRANDMA: *(Gets a wild look of recognition and yells)* Vivian Leigh! *(slaps Susie)* You stole that part from me! Stole it, I tell you!
(Immediately Randolph and Billy pull Grandma back.)
RANDOLPH: Mother! This is not Vivian Leigh!
BILLY: For heaven's sake, Father, is she still gone with the wind?
GRANDMA: Stole it, I tell you! She stole it!
(The maid comes running in.)
MAID: I'm sorry, Mr. Randolph. She wandered off when I was ... uh ... dusting the furniture.
RANDOLPH: Please, do not let this happen again! We're having a family celebration!
LOUISA: *(dramatically again)* At least trying to ... *(throws hands up and goes and drops onto couch)*
MAID: I promise, sir. I'm so sorry. *(to Grandma)* Come on, Miss Scarlett. We've no time to waste. Mr. Butler will be here any moment.

GRANDMA: Oh, my! *(turns and looks at Susie)* He's mine!
(Grandma and Maid exit)

TAMI-TINA: *(going to Susie)* Are you all right, Susie?

SUSIE: *(still rubbing her cheek)* I think so. Just a little surprised.

TINA-TAMI: Crazy old bat.

NILANSA: That crazy old bat is your grandmother. Try to be respectful. *(moves to wet bar and pours a drink)*

TINA-TAMI: Sorry—insane ancient flying mammal of the night.

NILANSA: Where do you get this dark sarcasm from?

(Bentley now appears at the top of the stairs.)

BUTLER: Hear ye! Hear ye, one and all! Presenting Master Bentley Magnum Cavanaugh, award winning action film actor, director, and producer, four-time winner …

BENTLEY: *(stopping the butler)* I think that's more than enough. And what is art, really? Can it honestly be labeled by prestigious awards and accolades? I think not! As Grandpa Linus always said, "What is an award but an overstatement of what is already obvious?"

(all do the Grandpa Linus salute)

NILANSA: Well, well, well, if it isn't my famous brother who has no time to get back to me when I have left message after message after message.

BENTLEY: Sorry. *(clears his throat)* Some of us are still at the apex of our careers.

NILANSA: What exactly are you insinuating?

BENTLEY: Really, Nilansa? Must I elaborate about the mother who is now riding the coattails of her twin daughters?

NILANSA: Of all the …

RANDOLPH: *(goes toward Bentley so he is standing between Bentley and couch where Tami-Tina has been consoling Susie)* Brother, sister ... please ... must we be so disagreeable when it's been so long since we were all last together like this?

BENTLEY: Sorry, Randolph. But of course you're right. *(to Nilansa)* Many apologies for not getting back to you about the prospect of the twins starring in my upcoming project.

TAMI-TINA: *(rushes toward Bentley, shoving Randolph out of the way)* What? Are you crazy, woman? You want to put us in one of *his* movies?

NILANSA: At some point, dear, you must make the transition to adulthood. I merely thought your Uncle Bentley might perhaps be a gentle stepping stone.

TINA-TAMI: Cool! Would we get to shoot guns?

TAMI-TINA: Ewwwwwww!

TINA-TAMI: Or stab someone? I would really love to murder someone on screen. That would be ridiculously awesome!

TAMI-TINA: Well, double ewwwwww ewwwwww! I am NOT going to carry a gun or a knife!

TINA-TAMI: *(jumps up from her chair)* I will, Uncle Bentley! I will! In fact, the movie could be about opposite twins. One is really clueless *(looks at her twin)* and the other is totally fed up with her. She gets a gun ... *and* a knife ... and hunts her down in cold blood and ...

NILANSA: Tina-Tami! That is not the kind of role I was looking for!

(Tina-Tami drops back down in the chair in a pout.)

LOUISA: Oh, my! Is it really the twins you're seeking a role for, or perhaps a little cameo for yourself.

NILANSA: Pipe it down, woman.

LOUISA: Maybe it's time to find a new agent.

TINA-TAMI: *(suddenly jumps out with hand formed as a gun)* I've got it! Jamie Bond, long lost daughter of famed agent 007, suddenly appears to avenge the murderous, and somewhat gruesome death of her father. *(begins to sing the Bond theme song, runs around stage, ends up pointing gun in Randolph's face.)* Did you murder my father?

RANDOLPH: What? *(raises hands in surrender)*

TAMI-TINA: Mother, make her stop!

NILANSA: Really, dear, you're upsetting your sister.

TINA-TAMI: *(points the gun at Tami-Tina)* Aha! It was you, wasn't it?

(Randolph sneaks back to his chair and script)

TAMI-TINA: Stop it! If I killed your father, then that means I killed my father!

TINA-TAMI: *(puts down her finger gun, pulls out a pretend rifle and cocks it)* The worst kind!

TAMI-TINA: *(screams)* Mother, make her stop!

BENTLEY: *(to Tina-Tami)* Oh, quite impressive. What kind of weapon do you have there.

TINA-TAMI: *(cocks her pretend rifle again)* 12-gauge. *(slowly pulls out another pretend weapon)* This ... is my M-16.

BENTLEY: Wo ...

TAMI-TINA: *(screaming)* No! Stop it!

NILANSA: Tami-Tina! Stop your incessant screaming! It's all pretend ... acting. What is it your drama coach always says when she gets under your skin like this? Oh, yes, go to your happy place. Go to your happy place, please!

TAMI-TINA: *(rubbing her temples)* Finding my happy place—finding my happy place. *(motions the next objects)* Rainbows and rivers ... butterflies and doves.

TINA-TAMI: *(mock shoots the butterflies and doves)* Boom! Boom!

TAMI-TINA: Ahhhh!

(twins should cause a noisy mayhem that Billy interrupts)

BILLY: Hello! *(everyone turns to him and quiets down)* Thank you. Before things get any more ... uncomfortable ... I was hoping we could settle into our rooms. *(Takes Susie's hand and leads her to their luggage)* Mother, where will Susie be staying, and I'll take her luggage on up.

LOUISA: Don't be ridiculous, dear. The butler will take the luggage up in just a jiffy.

BENTLEY: *(goes to Susie and takes her hand)* And who might this lovely young thing be?

BILLY: This is Susie.

NILANSA: William's fiancé'.

BENTLEY: Fiancé'? Really? I suppose that makes her off limits then.

NILANSA: She doesn't have the ring yet.

SUSIE: Actually, *(she holds up her finger)* I do. This engagement ring is just as binding in my heart as any wedding band.

NILANSA: *(briefly puts on thick reading glasses then takes Susie's hand and looks at the ring)* Wow, William, you counters must make great money.

BENTLEY: Yes, that's quite a rock there William.

BILLY: First of all, I'm not a counter, I'm an accountant. And second, it took her three years to say "yes." She deserved a nice "rock."

LOUISA: Three years? You've been seeing each other that long?

*(Fancy now appears at the top of the stairs—
walks down to center as butler announces)*

BUTLER: Hear ye! Hear ye, one and all! Presenting Miss Fancy Tansy Cavanaugh, award winning songstress of country music and star of the Broadway reprise of ***Annie's Got A Rifle.***

FANCY: Howdy, y'all! Long time, no see!

NILANSA: Fancy, darling, you look so ... quaint.

FANCY: Stop trying to be polite, Nilansa. It doesn't fit you. I am what I am what I am.

TAMI-TINA: I've never understood what that meant.

NILANSA: It means she's an odd cracker but she doesn't care.

FANCY: Oh, sister, sister, sister ... still can't handle the fact that my career is continuing to soar while yours has fallen into the good graces of your sweet little girls?

TAMI-TINA: We're not little!

TINA-TAMI: We're not sweet either. *(cocks her rifle)*

NILANSA: Oh, sister, still deluding ourselves that "southern music" is a legitimate art form?

FANCY: Deluded? Me? Let's see ... my latest award was ... oh ... last month! And yours was ... hmmm ... are we still just counting decades, or have we moved into centuries now?

NILANSA: Oh, I'm sorry, I wasn't referring to token awards, dear. I was speaking of genuine rewards given that actually bestow honor ... not clutter ... to one's shelf.

FANCY: *(balling her fist)* Okay, that does it! You've been asking for this a long time!

BENTLEY: *(running between the two women)* Girls, really! You must stop this incessant feuding!

BILLY: Fancy, I'd like you to meet my ... bride-to-be, Susie.

FANCY: *(raising her eyebrows)* Oh ... I didn't realize a wedding was in the planning. *(takes Susie's hand)* Well, don't you just seem like the sweetest thing ever!

SUSIE: Oh, goodness, how kind of you. It's a true pleasure to meet you. I make it a habit to watch my DVD of ***Annie's Got a Rifle*** at least once a month.

FANCY: A girl of obvious fine taste, William.

LOUISA: *(gets up from couch and goes to Susie, taking her arm)* Sweet Susie, why don't I take you on a personal tour of Wisteria before it gets any more dangerous in here?

BILLY: Mother, I can do that once we ...

LOUISA: No no, no ... I must be allowed to show my future daughter-in-law her inheritance. *(to Susie)* You will simply love the grounds here! We still have the tree house out back that William fell out of when he broke his sweet little legs.

(Susie looks nervously back at Billy as she exits with Louisa. He shrugs helplessly.)

TINA-TAMI: Cool! I didn't know that's how it happened. Wait! Aunt Louisa, show me where he fell! *(she runs out after them)*

TAMI-TINA: Not without me ... *(exits)*

(Randolph goes to the couch and begins to concentrate on his script again)

FANCY: *(going to bar for a drink)* You're marrying her? I just thought she was supposed to be a girlfriend.

NILANSA: *(goes to right chair)* Really, William, what do you even know about her?

BILLY: Okay, stop it. I know what you're all thinking.

BENTLEY: *(very seductively)* Bet you don't know what I'm thinking.

(Fancy goes to chair)

BILLY: Don't even go there, Bentley! This girl is different, I promise y'all that.

NILANSA: Y'all? Y'all? Did you pick up a copy of Fancy's hideous Southern English colloquialisms?

BILLY: I've lived in Alabama for six years. It just happens.

(While this conversation is going on, Grandma Kat comes in and sees the luggage Billy left at the bottom of the stairs. She takes Susie's and exits with it while no one notices.)

BENTLEY: That Susie does have a sweet, little accent, doesn't she? And a sweet little figure to match.

BILLY: Enough! She's not some bimbo who's hitched her wagon to a star.

NILANSA: This time ...

FANCY: William, you are so gullible when it comes to women.

NILANSA: Oh, my ... this from the woman who married Bobby Bill McDill? Country music's Cassanova!

FANCY: Oh, my ... are we counting failed marriages? Let's see—Fancy *(holds up one finger)*, one. Nilansa *(holds up five)* ...

BILLY: We've been together for three years. She had no idea who my family even was until two weeks ago.

BENTLEY: Keep telling yourself that, old boy. *(slaps Billy on back then goes to bar for a drink)*

BILLY: Okay, I'm not gonna stand here and try to defend myself to you people. *(goes to the luggage)* I'm going to settle in. *(notices Susie's bag is gone)* Did the Butler take Susie's bag on to the room?

NILANSA: Probably.

(Billy gets his bag and exits)
(Armando, the pool guy enters)

ARMANDO: *(with a very thick accent of some kind)* Pardon me, but I was looking for Mr. Randolph.

FANCY: Armando!

ARMANDO: Miss Fancy Tansy Cavanaugh ... you look as beautiful as ever.

NILANSA: *(stands and extends her hand to Armando)* Excuse me, but I never got the chance to thank you for ... well ... for all you did for me last time I was here.

ARMANDO: *(takes Nilansa's hand and kisses it)* Miss Nilansa Elizabeth Cavanaugh, it was my pleasure.

RANDOLPH: *(getting up from the couch)* Armando! Yes, my boy! Have you completed the little project we talked about earlier?

ARMANDO: Almost. I was hoping to speak with you alone for a moment.

RANDOLPH: But, of course. Right this way. *(they exit)*

FANCY: *(with a big smile)* Hello, Armando. Long time, no see.

BENTLEY: Really, Fancy, are you so desperate now that you're chasing after the hired help.

FANCY: I believe that is the pot calling the kettle black, Bentley. How many of the maids have you chased around Wisteria over the years?

(Bentley begins to count on his fingers then gives up after awhile.)

NILANSA: "Pot calling the kettle black" ... another of those darling colloquialisms. I know—why don't you and William and sweet little Susie order up three glasses of Mint-Julep and sit out on the porch swing. You could exchange stories about the *(obvious mock Southern accent)* blessin's and benefits of living in the hospitable, deep South.

FANCY: If you weren't a pitifully, old washed-up, has-been, I might be offended. But right now I'm afraid Mr. Armando has captivated my imagination.

NILANSA: He is quite good at that—capturing one's ... uh ... imagination.

FANCY: *(looking at Nilansa suspiciously)* What are you alluding to?

NILANSA: Oh, nothing. I'm just saying that Armando can be very ... accommodating.

FANCY: In your dreams.

NILANSA: Most assuredly.

BENTLEY: You two are nauseating.

(Randolph and Armando enter)

RANDOLPH: Thank you, Armando.

ARMANDO: I will get on that right away, Mr. Randolph. It should be completed by this afternoon. *(walks by the ladies and nods respectfully)* Ladies. *(they melt and he exits)*

FANCY: *(fanning her face)* Be still, my heart.

NILANSA: Fancy, dear, you are too much of a child for the smoldering Armando. He needs a real woman ... a more mature and experienced soul.

FANCY: Well, you sure fit the bill for experience ... a bit overused even.

BENTLEY: Oh, please, you two. I can't stomach much more of this.

(Billy enters)

BILLY: Does anyone know where Mother planned to put Susie?

NILANSA: I would assume the west tower.

FANCY: Me too ... that's usually where first time guests stay.

BENTLEY: *(dreamily)* Ah, yes ... I remember many firsts in the west tower.

BILLY: I thought so too, but her luggage wasn't there. *(to Randolph)* Father, do you know where Susie's supposed to sleep?

RANDOLPH: *(engrossed in his script again)* No idea, son.

BILLY: *(scratching his head)* Strange.

NILANSA: Strange? Let's talk about strange.

FANCY: Yes, my thoughts exactly. Susie would be what number in the long line of girls you've brought to Wisteria?

BILLY: Can you not leave this alone? I've told you that this whole thing is different. Susie and I have dated for three years, and she had no idea who my family was.

NILANSA: She certainly seems to know who we all are now.

BILLY: Well, she knew who you all were ... just not that you were my family.

BENTLEY: *(comes out from behind bar)* So, you dated that sweet dumpling for three years and never came clean about your family? *(slaps Billy on the back)* I'm impressed! I didn't realize you could be so deceptive—requires a bit of an imagination to hold out that kind of truth for so long. *(he joins Randolph on the couch)*

(Grandma Kat walks through the room behind them all wearing the dress and hat that Susie wore to the park in the first scene)

FANCY: The only imagination I'm having right now involves me, a pool, and a pool cleaning guy.

NILANSA: Must be a big imagination. I thought we'd already been through this, sister dear—you aren't quite woman enough for the pool cleaning guy.

FANCY: *(balling her fist)* Would you like me to show you in a very unimaginative and clear way just how "strong" of a woman I really am?

BILLY: Would you two stop? This is just what I don't need—for Susie to walk in and see the two aunts I was raised with carrying on a fist fight over the pool guy.

NILANSA: Oh, come on, William. The best thing we could do for you is scare little Susie off.

FANCY: I can't believe you've fallen for this trick all over again.

BILLY: She's not like that, I tell you! Why is it so hard for all of you to believe that someone could actually love me for me ... and not because of all of you?

NILANSA: It's called your "track record".

BENTLEY: There's one way to find out for sure.

BILLY: And how do you suppose that?

BENTLEY: Let me have a go at her.

BILLY: No way! You better not lay a hand on her!

FANCY: If she loves you like you claim, surely she wouldn't fall for Bentley's charms ... and looks ...

NILANSA: ... and resume'.

BILLY: You leave her alone!

(The twins come in with lollipops)

BENTLEY: Where'd you get candy?

TAMI-TINA: The cook. She always gives us candy.

BENTLEY: Really? Why?

TAMI-TINA: Because she thinks we're sweet.

TINA-TAMI: ... and she thinks we're still six years old.

BENTLEY: Rather tall for six year-olds, aren't you?

TINA-TAMI: We never said she was brilliant.

(Louisa and Susie enter)

LOUISA: And that, dear Susie, was how William wet his pants at the White House! *(laughs)*

BILLY: You did *not* tell her that story, Mother.

SUSIE: *(going to Billy and taking his hands)* Oh, it's cute, Billy. You're mother's told me so many things about you when you were young. It's nice to finally have the gaps filled in.

BENTLEY: *(standing)* Perhaps I should take you on a tour. Bet I know some places around here that Louisa never knew existed.

BILLY: *(stepping between Bentley and Susie)* No! If anyone else takes Susie on a tour, it will be me.

(Grandma Kat walks in)

SUSIE: *(recognizing the clothes)* My dress! My hat!

LOUISA: What, dear?

BILLY: Grandma Kat, did you take Susie's luggage?

GRANDMA KAT: *(looking wildly at Susie again)* Vivian!

SUSIE: My mistake! Not my clothes! Looks lovely on you, Miss Katherine. I'm sure you'll get the role over me.

GRANDMA KAT: Ha! *(exits)*

BILLY: *(to Louisa)* Mother, those were Susie's clothes. Could you please get someone to find her luggage?

LOUISA: Oh, dear. Where is that maid? She's supposed to keep Grandma from doing this kind of tomfoolery.

(Suddenly a scream pierces through from offstage. The maid comes running in.)

MAID: Mr. Randolph! Mr. Randolph!

RANDOLPH: *(standing quickly)* What is it, dear girl?

MAID: *(very dramatically, obviously over-acting)* I'm afraid ... I'm afraid ...

RANDOLPH: Well, spit it out, child!

MAID: I'm afraid there's been a ... a ... a murder!

LOUISA: Oh, my stars, no! *(She faints and Billy catches her)*

NILANSA: *(to Louisa who is looking with one eye)* Oh, no you don't, lady. *(dramatically)* A murder? Here at Wisteria? I don't believe it! Who was it, girl?

MAID: It was the handsome, yet somewhat tortured soul of the *(she pauses)* pool cleaning guy.

NILANSA: *(excessively dramatic)* No! No! No! *(faints incredibly and Bentley catches her)*

FANCY: The pool cleaning guy? Are you kidding me? No! It can't be! *(runs from the room in crying torment)*

TINA-TAMI: Where is he? Is he floating in the pool? I wanna see! *(runs out)*

TAMI-TINA: Ewwwwwww! *(gets a look of excitement)* Me too! *(runs out)*

BENTLEY: Shouldn't someone call the police ... or something?

RANDOLPH: Splendid idea, my boy! I guess that kind of thinking comes from years of making films filled with murder and suspense. I suppose I should be the one to do that. I'll make the call from the study ... seems more dramatic that way. A call from the parlor would be ...

BENTLEY: Drab.

RANDOLPH: Exactly! Very well, then ... to the study!
(leaves)

BENTLEY: *(drags Nilansa to the couch)* I'd like to have a look at the poor fellow myself. It's not often I see a real murder.

(Bentley leaves)

SUSIE: Billy, what is going on?

BILLY: *(still holding Louisa)* Welcome to Wisteria.

BLACKOUT

ACT ONE
Scene Three

SCENE: *(Later that evening in the guest bedroom. Billy and Susie are sitting on a bed as he consoles her over the events surrounding the murder. A dressing bench is opposite them on the stage.)*

SUSIE: *(wiping tears, very upset)* Billy, I don't know if I've ever seen anything so horrid. There was the body floating in the pool, then there was all the police, and then they dragged him out ... and ... and *(she breaks into sobs)*

BILLY: I really don't think there's a need to be so upset by it.

SUSIE: What is it with you people?! A man was dead in the pool! Other than your mother and Aunt Nilansa fainting, the only other emotion I saw out there was morbid curiosity! *(mocking Randolph)* "I suppose I should call the police ... I'll do it from the study ... it would be drab to do it from the parlor." How can you not be overwrought with anguish about this? A man just died!

BILLY: I tried to tell you my family was ... different.

SUSIE: Different? What I saw down there wasn't different! It was flat out weird—borderline insanity!

BILLY: Agreed. *(sighs)* At least you got your luggage back.

SUSIE: Barely ... I would have let her have it except for the fact that I've sweated up a storm today from all the anxiety this place has put me through! I would be unfit to be around from the stench had I not showered and changed.

BILLY: I'm sorry. I grew up in this, Susie. In my family there's a fine line between reality and imagination—the dramatic and the normal.

SUSIE: An extremely fine line. Billy, there was a dead body in the pool and everyone just ... just ... *(sobs again)*

BILLY: Can you see now why I wanted to get away from all this? Can you see why I didn't want to bring you here ... didn't want to expose you to this craziness? I grew up thinking I was really, really weird—then I went to college.

SUSIE: I imagine that was quite a shocker for you.

BILLY: You have no idea. It was like I was released from prison. I remember my first normal conversation. My roommate walked into the dorm room and said, "Hi, I'm Spencer." He looked around the room and then added, "I'm glad we don't have bunk beds. I was really worried about that." I didn't know what to do, Susie. At first I thought I should stand on the desk and yell, *(dramatically)* "My name is William Desmond Cavanaugh, and I will be studying alongside you here at this glorious institution of higher learning!"

SUSIE: You didn't, did you?

BILLY: No, I just stuck out my hand and said, "Hi, I'm Billy. Which side of the room do you prefer?" I'd never been called "Billy" in my life, but at that moment, I knew I was never going back to being William Desmond again. I was just Billy Cavanaugh—plain, non-phenomenal, Billy.

SUSIE: Oh, Billy—there's nothing plain at ...

LOUISA: *(off stage)* Yoo hoo! Knock, knock! Is everyone decent?

BILLY: Mother! Of course, we're decent!

(Louisa enters)

LOUISA: You never know these days. I just wanted to check on our special little guest here at Wisteria Mansion and make sure she was comfy and cozy and ready for beddy-bye.

SUSIE: Oh, goodness, yes, Miss Louisa. *I'm* just fine, but how are *you*?

LOUISA: *(looking confused)* How am I about what, dear?

SUSIE: You know—down there ... what happened today ... when you fainted after the ... well ... after the murder.

LOUISA: *(with energy)* That was quite exciting, wasn't it!

SUSIE: *(a little irritated at her lack of being upset)* You passed out. I just wondered if you were still feeling a little light-headed.

LOUISA: My stars, no, dear! I haven't time for all that tonight. We'll pick that mess back up in the morning.

BILLY: It did kind of ruin dinner, Mother. I had hoped we could have an uneventful visit.

LOUISA: *(laughs)* Wisteria? Uneventful? Ha! William— you should have been a comedian!

SUSIE: *(confused)* So, you are better then?

LOUISA: Dear, dear child ... as Grandfather Linus always said, "There's nothing like a little catastrophe to bring all of the squirrels out of their little trees!"

(Linus salute—even Susie attempts it)

BILLY: I think the saying was, "There's nothing like a catastrophe to help distinguish the squirrels from the nuts."

(Grandma Kat wanders in still wearing Susie's clothes)

GRANDMA KAT: And you, sir, are no squirrel! You're no gentleman either!

BILLY: Apparently not, but I'm most definitely a nut for thinking I could come back here and have a normal visit with my family.

(Maid comes in)

MAID: There you are, Miss Scarlett! I've been looking all over for you! How do you keep slipping away like that?

GRANDMA KAT: And you, miss, are no squirrel either!

MAID: How nice of you to notice, Miss Scarlett. But seriously, you must stop sneaking away.

GRANDMA KAT: Tara is large place, Prissy … a large place.

MAID: Yes, ma'am. And it's time to get you into that large bed of yours.

(Randolph enters)

RANDOLPH: Ah, there you all are! I've been searching high and low for my missing family! Having a party in here, are we?

BILLY: No, sir. I was just saying "goodnight" to Susie and then people began showing up.

RANDOLPH: Ah … excellent! Glad I found you all then! I was on my way for a nightcap, but I suppose I could have the bottle brought in here.

LOUISA: Marvelous idea, darling! Should I page the butler?

GRANDMA KAT: Butler? Rhett Butler? He's here? *(panics)* Oh, Prissy! I have nothing to wear! What'll I do? What'll I do?

(Grandma Kat runs out, Maid follows,
Nilansa enters, wine in hand)

NILANSA: What's all the commotion about in here?

(Everyone welcomes her in.
Billy throws his hands up in exasperation)

LOUISA: We were about to page the butler and have him bring in a bottle.

NILANSA: Delightful!

BILLY: I'd really rather you didn't. *(they all look confused)*

LOUSIA: Why, dear?

BILLY: Susie and I don't drink.

LOUISA: Why ... dear?

BILLY: We just don't choose to indulge in alcohol consumption.

LOUISA: Yes ... why?

SUSIE: We prefer life to be simpler ... pure ... pristine. Alcohol clouds your thinking ... clouds your emotions. We don't want to dull our senses—we want to embrace them—every moment of them.

*(Randolph and Louise think on the words,
then begin clapping and yelling, "Bravo!")*

RANDOLPH: *(impressed)* Well said, dear girl! Almost makes one want to give it a try!

(Bentley enters and all greet him)

BENTLEY: Well, well, well ... seems everyone had the same idea I did—can't get enough of William's sweet little Susie, huh? Thought I'd check on her and make sure she didn't have any unmet needs.

LOUISA: How very thoughtful of you, Bentley.

BILLY: *(sarcastically)* Yes ... quite.

RANDOLPH: Bentley! Welcome, old boy! Come in and join us!

LOUISA: Yes! We were about to round up a bottle.

BILLY: Okay! Enough! *(everyone gets quiet and stares)* We are not having a party, or a nightcap, or a bottle of anything in Susie's room.

BENTLEY: I suppose a spirited game of Charades would be out of the question then.

LOUISA: Oh, yes! Charades!

RANDOLPH: Magnificent suggestion, Bentley!

NILANSA: Oh, let me go first! I have a good one!

*(everyone gets excited and gives her their attention
as Nilansa hands her wine glass to Susie)*

LOUISA: What fun!

*(Randolph and Louisa sit on small bench opposite bed,
Bentley stands behind them)*

(Nilansa does the motions for "book.")
RANDOLPH: It's a book!
(Nilansa nods and claps her hands. She then holds up two fingers.)
BENTLEY: Peace!
(Nilansa shakes her head.)
LOUISA: A book about peace? Hmmm ...
RANDOLPH: "War and Peace"!
BENTLEY: Of course! Very good, Randolph. I don't read much myself ... haven't the time really.
(Nilansa shakes her head furiously.)
LOUISA: Not about peace? Okay ... it's a "V"! "V" for victory!
RANDOLPH: A book about victory, you say?
(Nilansa shakes her head in frustration.)
BILLY: *(stands frustrated)* No ... what she means is that the title of the book has two words! *(drops down on bed)*
(Nilansa nods frantically now.)
LOUISA: *(laughing)* Of course! How silly of us!
(Nilansa holds up two fingers again, then she holds up one finger.)
BENTLEY: Wait a minute. Have you changed books on us? Now it has only one word?
BILLY: *(stands again)* No! The book has two words in the title. Now she's going to give you the clue for what the first word in the title is. *(drops down again)*
BENTLEY: Why didn't she say so?
NILANSA: Because it's "Charades", you ninny!
LOUISA: Touchy, aren't we?
(Nilansa gives Louisa a scowl then begins the whole process again. She makes the "book" motion.)
RANDOLPH: Yes, it's a book.
(Nilansa holds up two fingers.)
BENTLEY: There are two words in the title of this book.
(Nilansa now holds up one finger.)

LOUISA: First word in the title is …?
> *(Nilansa now sticks her hands out forming "C's" with her thumbs and forefingers, looking a bit like crab pinchers.)*

BENTLEY: You're a crab!
> *(Nilansa shakes her head. Emphasizes her fingers again.)*

LOUISA: You're not a crab—you're some other kind of creature?
> *(Nilansa shakes her head, continues motion.)*

RANDOLPH: Wait! I've got it! You're not a crab! You're a lobster!
> *(Nilansa shakes her head getting angry, but continues with the fingers.)*

LOUISA: You're a very mad lobster! *(Nilansa shakes her head more furious.)* A mad, angry lobster!

BENTLEY: Oh! I've got it! Red Lobster! The name of the book is Red Lobster!

NILANSA: You imbecile! That is the name of an eating establishment! Not the name of a book. This *(she shows her finger motions again)* has nothing to do with a crustacean of any kind!

LOUISA: I thought you weren't supposed to talk, dear?

NILANSA: *(furiously)* Then pay attention! *(This time she makes a motion meaning "big.")*

BENTLEY: Big? Huge? Large?
> *(Nilansa now nods and makes the big motion again then does the fingers and thumbs.)*

LOUISA: Oh, oh, oh! I get it! Little!
> *(Nilansa nods and claps. She then points to her nose to indicate the correct answer.)*

RANDOLPH: Nose! Little nose! The title of the book is "Little Nose."
> *(Nilansa shakes her head.)*

BENTLEY: Ah … but it has something to do with a nose!

LOUISA: Barbra Streisand! It's one of those Streisand books!

RANDOLPH: Oh ... oh ... "Silly Girl" or "Silly Lady"?

BILLY: *(again stands)* It has nothing to do with a nose! When she touches her nose that means you've got the answer correct! You're "right on". *(touches his nose as he says "right on.")*

LOUISA: Oh! Of course! Marvelous, then. Please continue, Nilansa.

> *(Obviously worn out, Nilansa makes the "small" motion again.)*

BENTLEY: Little. Little what?

> *(Nilansa now begins to act out "Women.")*

LOUISA: Little Barbra Streisand!

NILANSA: This has nothing to do with Barbra Streisand! It's a book! Not a movie! Not a song!

BENTLEY: Goodness ... are we having fun yet, Nilansa? I thought this was supposed to be a game.

NILANSA: *(almost yelling)* It is a game! But it obviously requires more than half a brain for it to actually be enjoyable!

BILLY: *(sarcastically)* I'm having the time of my life. *(to Susie)* Aren't you?

RANDOLPH: Be patient, everyone. We haven't played in a while. We're just having to get our groove back on.

LOUISA: *(laughing)* Oh, my, Randolph! I'm not exactly certain I ever had any groove to begin with.

NILANSA: Okay, okay, okay ... back to the game.

BENTLEY: Right. Now, what was the first word again?

BILLY & SUSIE: Little!

BENTLEY: Oh, yes! What's next, Nilansa?

> *(Nilansa does the woman thing again.)*

RANDOLPH: You're obviously some kind of female.

> *(Nilansa nods frantically and touches her nose again.)*

BENTLEY: Again with the nose? I thought it had nothing to do with a nose!

NILANSA: It doesn't! This means you're guessing the right word! Randolph guessed "female"! The second word in the title has something to do with a female!

LOUSIA: You keep talking, dear. You're not very good at this game.

NILANSA: *I'm* not very good at this game?! *I'm* not very good?! Are you kidding me?

BENTLEY: Okay, I'm confused. Is the word "nose" anywhere in the title?

BILLY & SUSIE: No!

BENTLEY: All right ... I'm on the same page now. Continue, Nilansa.

NILANSA: Augh! Okay, let's go through this one more time. *(She does the book motion.)*

LOUISA: For crying out loud, we know it's a book, Nilansa!

(Nilansa gives Louisa the evil eye, then holds up two fingers.)

RANDOLPH: Yes, yes ... there are two words in the title.

(She holds up one finger.)

BENTLEY: First word is ... *(Nilansa does the finger and thumb motion again)* ... crab ... no! Lobster! No ... wait ... little! *(Nilansa nods and starts to touch her nose, then stops immediately.)* Yes! The first word is "little."

(Nilansa holds up two fingers now.)

LOUISA: Second word?

(Nilansa nods and does the woman again.)

RANDOLPH: A female ...

(Nilansa nods and continues.)

BENTLEY: Mae West! Little Mae West!

(Nilansa shakes her head.)

LOUISA: Little ... little ... little females ...

(Nilansa now goes around and points at all the women in the room.)

RANDOLPH: All the little females!

NILANSA: No! Another word for female!

BENTLEY: Girl?

NILANSA: No!

RANDOLPH: Lady?

NILANSA: No!

LOUISA: You really should stop talking or we're going to have to start subtracting points.

BILLY: *(jumps up exasperated)* Women! The title of the book is "Little Women"!

NILANSA: *(touching her nose with an exaggerated point)* Yes! "Little Women"!

RANDOLPH: That was a book? I thought that was a movie?

LOUISA: It was a movie ... several movies in fact. No wonder we couldn't guess it! *(to Nilansa)* You really should pay more attention to your facts.

NILANSA: It was a book too!

BENTLEY: Really? How silly. Why do they keep doing that ... writing books about movies?

BILLY: It was a book first! Written many years ago! The movies ... all of them ... were made based on the book!

LOUISA: Hmmm ... imagine that! *(to Nilansa)* I'm impressed, dear, that you knew that. How stunning!

(Grandma and Maid enter just as Louisa says "How stunning"...Grandma is now dressed in Scarlett O'hara attire and responds as though Louisa has complimented her)

GRANDMA KAT: Why, thank you!

RANDOLPH: That was quite invigorating! It's been years since we've had a *good* game of Charades.

SUSIE: *(almost sarcastically)* Would there actually be such a thing as a *bad* game of Charades with you people?

(They all look at her in shock and disgust)

BILLY: *(shaking his head)* Oh, boy ...

SUSIE: What? What did I say?

LOUISA: *(putting her hand to her head)* No, I will not faint again ... I will stay strong.

RANDOLPH: *(Going to her side immediately)* Yes, darling, yes ... that's right, dear Louisa, stay strong. Let me help you out. *(guiding her to leave)* Perhaps we'll take that nightcap alone.

LOUSIA: Yes ... perhaps ... perhaps.

NILANSA: *(to Susie)* I can't believe ... how could you ... *(slowly begins to burst into emotional tears and starts to exit, then grabs her glass from Susie and leaves)*

BENTLEY: *(trying to be tough and in control, but having a hard time)* Well ... uh ... yes ... I suppose I should be ... *(sniffs)* ... somewhere else. *(leaves)*

GRANDMA KAT: Home. I'll go home. And I'll think of some way to get him back. After all ... tomorrow is another day.

MAID: Yes, Miss Scarlett. *(glares at Susie as she escorts Grandma from the room)*

SUSIE: What on earth did I say, Billy?

BILLY: Grandpa Linus ... passed away ... during a game of Charades.

SUSIE: *(stunned and embarrassed)* Well, did he happen to have any last words?

BILLY: *(nodding)* He looked at Grandma Kat and said, *(opening his hands like a book)* "This, blasted woman, is a book! This *(does the movie motion)* is a movie!" *(pauses)* And then he just fell over ... dead.

SUSIE: *(sighs deeply)* Wow. *(shakes her head then does the Linus salute)*

BLACKOUT

ACT TWO
Scene One

SCENE: *It is the next morning back in the parlor of Wisteria Mansion. Susie comes in alone and begins looking at the awards on the shelf. While she is speaking, the butler comes in, dusting off his clothes, preparing to head to his spot at the top of the stairs. He eventually notices Susie and heads over to announce her, but she has no idea he is there.*

SUSIE: So, this is what an Oscar looks like. *(She picks it up and puts it back, then picks up an Emmy.)* An Emmy award—can't believe I'm holding one in my own hands. Oh, look! This is the year Billy was born! I've seen the reruns—it was a good year. Louisa was pregnant and clumsy, so every skit was hilarious. *(She then gets a Grammy.)* Look at this—their very own Grammy for album of the year. And to think, Billy can't carry a tune. *(She pauses and the butler appears unaware that she is in the room. She speaks next line and he runs up to her.)* I wonder if he was even in the studio?
BUTLER: Hear, ye! Hear ye …
SUSIE: *(screaming from surprise)* What are you doing?
BUTLER: I am announcing you, Miss.
SUSIE: There's nobody here!
BUTLER: But, you are, Miss.
SUSIE: And I know exactly who I am! Why are you sneaking around anyway?

BUTLER: I believe, Miss, that *you* would be the one sneaking around. I was merely headed to my post—the place where I belong. You were touching major awards.

(Billy enters.)

BILLY: *(moving with relief to Susie and startles her again)* There you are!

BUTLER: Hear, ye! Hear, ye, one and all ...

BILLY: Please ... stop.

BUTLER: But I am to announce you, sir.

BILLY: But there's no reason to. The only person I want to see right now is standing here beside me. Your announcing would be pointless.

BUTLER: Very well, sir. I shall retire to my post then. *(he heads up the stairs)*

BILLY: I went to your room and knocked and knocked, then I started calling you. I finally went on in, and when I saw you weren't there, I began to panic.

SUSIE: Were you afraid someone had killed me too?

BILLY: Well ... no ... just afraid that you had left in the middle of night.

SUSIE: Not that the thought didn't occur to me ... several times in fact ... but no. I wouldn't just walk out like that and leave you here with them ... alone.

BILLY: I'm so sorry about all this, Susie.

SUSIE: *(putting her hand up to stop him)* You tried to warn me. This is one of those things you have to experience to believe. *(she puts award back on shelf)* Do you realize the amount of accolade contained on this shelf?

BILLY: Or insanity ...

SUSIE: I was thinking, Billy—and please don't take this the wrong way—but as much as I would like to have a family someday, I don't really know that I want to be responsible for ... perpetuating ... this particular gene pool.

(Fancy appears with a deep wail.)

FANCY: Ohhhhhhhh!

BUTLER: Hear, ye! Hear, ye, one and all! Presenting Miss Fancy Tansy Cavanaugh, award winning songstress and ...

FANCY: *(motioning him to stop)* Not now, not now. I haven't the stomach or heart to think of my own shallow accomplishments in this meager life. *(She walks over to the couch and throws herself on it, weeping.)* Armando! Armando! Why? Why you, sweet man?

BILLY: Who's Armando?

FANCY: *(momentarily pulling out of her drama)* You really should come around more often. That's the name of the pool guy who was ... murdered! *(She begins weeping again.)*

BILLY: Oh, that's right.

SUSIE: *(sitting beside Fancy trying to offer comfort)* I'm so sorry. Were you two close?

FANCY: *(stunned)* Exactly what are you accusing me of?

SUSIE: Nothing ... you just seem so ... distraught.

FANCY: Armando was a wonderful, sensitive soul ... a caring man with a tender ... well, he was very nice. He's worked here for many years. I'm surprised you don't know him, William.

BILLY: I didn't realize his name was Edwardo.

FANCY: Armando! His name is ... was ... Armando! *(begins weeping again)*

(Louisa walks in distressed, carrying an apron.)

BUTLER: Hear ye! Hear ye, one and all! Presenting Ms. Louisa Henrietta Cavanaugh, award winning ...

LOUISA: Not now! We have no time for this! Another tragedy has occurred!

(The butler shakes his head in disgust.)

SUSIE: *(jumps up from couch)* O my gosh! Has someone else been murdered?

LOUISA: No, dear, it's even worse than that!

BILLY: *(throwing his hands up in exasperation)* What now?

LOUISA: The cook has walked out! She said the death of the pool guy was the last straw and she just walked out! What are we going to do?

BILLY: Mother, that's not a tragedy. You just hire someone else.

LOUISA: But she was like a member of the family! *(looking sadly at Billy)* It would seem all my family is leaving me! All of them! *(throws herself on the couch with Fancy and begins to sob also)*

(Bentley enters)

BUTLER: Hear ye! Hear ye, one and all! Presenting Master Bentley Magnum Cavanaugh. *(Bentley shakes his head to stop him.)* I figured as much.

BENTLEY: What time will breakfast be served?

(Louisa weeps louder)

SUSIE: The cook quit.

BENTLEY: Oh, my ... how distressing. *(raises an eyebrow at Susie)* Perhaps Miss Susie could join me in the kitchen and we could see what kind of adventures might be cooked up in there.

BILLY: *(stepping beside Susie)* Susie's not the adventurous type.

BENTLEY: And how would you know, young William? Perhaps the idea of adventure has never been presented to her in such a ... pleasurable way.

SUSIE: *(taking Billy's arm)* I've had more than enough adventure the past 24 hours to last me a lifetime, thank you.

BENTLEY: My dear, you haven't even touched the surface of adventure.

(The twins enter dressed in black.)

TAMI-TINA: Ewwwww! I hate black! I can't believe you made me wear this!

BUTLER: Hear ye! Hear ye, one and all!

TWINS: *(yelling together)* Shut up!

(The Butler folds his arms in disgust.)

TINA-TAMI: This isn't a fashion statement. We should wear black today in honor of the pool guy's death.
(Both Fancy and Louisa begin wailing again.)
BENTLEY: Oh, yes, forgot all about that. We did have a murder, didn't we?
TAMI-TINA: Uh ... yes!
BENTLEY: I was so hungry I suppose it all just slipped my mind.
SUSIE: A murder slipped your mind? Is every one of you crazy?
TINA-TAMI: *(pulls out a really big knife)* Now, about that role in one of your movies, Uncle Bentley.
TAMI-TINA: Ahhhhh! Put it away!
(Nilansa enters)
NILANSA: Tina-Tami! Stop that! I told you not to bring props home from the set! *(goes to bar for a drink)*
BUTLER: Hear ye! Hear ye ...
NILANSA and TWINS: Shut up!
(Butler is disgusted)
TINA-TAMI: It's not a prop. I bought it off the internet.
NILANSA: Oh, very well then. Carry on.
(The maid enters. She looks up to the butler who is standing with his arms folded and snaps her fingers.)
BUTLER: *(unenthusiastically)* Hear ye ... Hear ye ... it's the maid.
MAID: *(rolling her eyes she walks over to Louisa and dramatically announces)* Miss Louisa, I don't know how to cook.
LOUISA: *(bossy as she forces the apron over the cook's neck)* You are the hired help, dear girl. It is your job to "figure it out" ... if you value your position.
(The maid leaves in frustration.)
TINA-TAMI: *(to Bentley)* Maybe I could be a Ninja warrior or something? Like a secret assassin! *(she slings the knife around toward her sister)*
TAMI-TINA: Ewwww! Stop it! Mother, make her stop!
NILANSA: Don't slice at your sister, dear.

TAMI-TINA: Besides, you can't possibly expect Uncle Bentley to give you a starring role in one of his movies just because you can sling a knife around.

TINA-TAMI: Hey! Doesn't matter. I don't need a big role—I just need to NOT be joined to you at the hip for the rest of my life. Anyway, it's like Grandpa Linus always said, "Great talent can make a Chihuahua seem like a Pit Bull."

(Everyone does the Linus salute.)

TAMI-TINA: That's not what he said! He said, "Great talent can make a Mackerel out of a minnow."

(Linus salute again ...)

TINA-TAMI: Whatever ... you can be a flopping fish if you want. I choose the fighting, biting dog.

(Randolph enters.)

BUTLER: Oh, looky! It's Randy!

RANDOLPH: *(looking at the butler sternly)* Excuse me, sir?

BUTLER: *(embarrassed)* So sorry, Mr. Cavanaugh. It's been a bit of a rough morning.

RANDOLPH: I should say so. Where's breakfast? I went into the dining room and ...

LOUISA: *(wailing again)* Cooky quit!

RANDOLPH: *(walks down to couch)* She did what? Why on earth?

BENTLEY: Apparently the murder of the pool guy got to her.

FANCY: Armando! Why can't any of you call him by his name! Am I the only one who cares the man was murdered here right under our noses!

(The maid enters with a tray of Pop-Tarts. She looks up to the butler.)

BUTLER: Hear ye! Hear ye, one and all! Breakfast is served!

(They move to take a pastry.)

LOUISA: Dear, girl, you said you couldn't cook. These look simply delightful!

TWINS: Pop-tarts!

BENTLEY: Tarts! Marvelous! What a lovely breakfast you've whipped up! *(suggestively to the maid)* Sweets from the sweet.

MAID: Oh, Mr. Bentley, it was nothing ... really.

BENTLEY: Don't sell your talents short.

MAID: *(obviously flirting)* Well, if you say so.

RANDOLPH: Quite tasty, they are.

FANCY: *(still grieving)* How can you all eat when ... Armando is dead!?

BENTLEY: Ah, yes ... the murder. I keep forgetting about all that. *(still noticing the maid)* It's easy to forget the horrid when surrounded by such unspoiled beauty.

NILANSA: Oh, please ...

LOUISA: However did you make these, dear?

MAID: I didn't. Armando eats them ... ate them ... all the time. I went to his bungalow and found several boxes in his pantry. I told you—I don't cook.

NILANSA: *(offensively to the maid)* What were *you* doing in his bungalow?

LOUISA: Do you think he might possibly have anything in there for lunch?

FANCY: *(emotionally distraught)* Can we please honor Armando's memory and stop ransacking his living quarters for food? What is wrong with you people?

LOUISA: *(emotional herself)* All I am trying to do as the mistress of this house is take care of these inhabitants and guests! The world doesn't stop just because a pool guy gets axed!

FANCY: Stop calling him "the pool guy"! His name is ... was ... Armando!

LOUISA: For heaven's sake, dear! If there is food in the man's bungalow, we desperately need it! What good is it if the rest of us starve to death mourning his memory!

(everyone gets loud in agreement)

SUSIE: *(yelling to get everyone's attention)* Hello! *(they all look to her)* I can cook. Let me see what's in the kitchen, and I'll try to pull something together for dinner.

LOUISA: Oh, we have a menu already, dear.

BILLY: Mother! She isn't the hired cook. She shouldn't be cooking at all! We came here to visit family, not to work.

MAID: Oh, no you don't! *(She quickly puts the apron around Susie's neck.)* She volunteered—she's cooking! This is not my area of expertise!

SUSIE: It's no problem—really. *(to the maid)* If you'll show me around the kitchen I'll see what I can manage to rustle up.

BILLY: Susie …

SUSIE: Please, let me cook. That's one thing that's down to earth and normal here.

MAID: *(seductively)* Perhaps Mr. Bentley should join us. He knows his way around the kitchen quite well.

BENTLEY: *(a bit offended)* And apparently you know your way around the pool guy's bungalow quite well.

(Grandma Kat comes running in toward Susie. She is still wearing Susie's hat.)

GRANDMA KAT: Oh, Vivian! There you are!

SUSIE: *(puts out her arms in defense)* Grandma Kat, I am not Vivian Leigh!

GRANDMA KAT: Dear, dear, deluded Vivian. *(takes Susie's hand and gently rubs it)* Congratulations, you will make a marvelous Scarlett.

SUSIE: *(not sure how to respond)* You really think so?

GRANDMA KAT: No, dear, but Clark Gable has awful halitosis. I'm afraid my constitution is too fragile to deal with that.

SUSIE: Oh … okay.

GRANDMA KAT: *(said in passing to the others)* Horrible script. That movie will never go anywhere.

SUSIE: *(to Billy)* I'm not sure if I was just complimented or insulted.

(Bentley cuts in and takes the arms of the maid and Susie.)

BENTLEY: Shall we make our way to the kitchen, ladies?

MAID: Indeed.

BILLY: *(protesting Bentley's accompanying them)* Hang on there …

SUSIE: Billy, it's all right. I'm going to cook. What could possibly happen in a kitchen?

BILLY: You don't know Bentley!

BENTLEY: A problem we shall soon rectify. *(on his way out)* Have you heard about the time I was filming at the Taj Mahal with Angelina?

(They exit.)

TAMI-TINA: You think the maid might give us candy?

TINA-TAMI: I think the maid will give us anything we want if she knows we know how often she visits that little bungalow out back.

(They giggle and run out.)

NILANSA: Worried, William?

BILLY: Not for the reasons you think.

NILANSA: I'm sure sweet, little Susie won't be taken in by the wiles of big, bad Bentley as long as the maid and the twins are around.

BILLY: Bentley's only one of many worries at the moment. *(to his parents)* What is the deal with the murder? Is anyone investigating it? Why are there no detectives here asking questions? Obviously someone on this compound is responsible and we're all walking around as if life carries on as usual.

LOUISA: Compound? You make it sound like a prison.

RANDOLPH: This is an estate, William, or is your mind so clouded by this Sissy Smith that you can't even remember your roots properly?

BILLY: Susie! Her name is Susie! You can remember every word in a Shakespearean play, but you can't remember something as simple as "Susie"?

NILANSA: A little too simple, don't you think?

BILLY: What is that supposed to mean?

NILANSA: When is the last time you actually heard someone called "Susie"?

RANDOLPH: Interesting point, sister. Not a common name of late.

LOUISA: Oh, my—now that you mention it, that is a rather unusual name for someone from the South. Don't they usually have double names like Betty-Sue or Mary-Anne?

BILLY: Are you kidding? Susie? You all think there's something doubtful about the name "Susie"?

NILANSA: And then you add "Smith" to the combination and it's downright suspicious.

(Grandma Kat comes running through carrying a stuffed dog.)

GRANDMA KAT: Follow the yellow brick road.

RANDOLPH: What did she just say?

GRANDMA KAT: *(coming up to Randolph)* Follow the yellow brick road.

RANDOLPH: Follow the yellow brick road?

GRANDMA KAT: Yes! Follow the yellow brick road!

(Grandma Kat runs out)

LOUISA: What was that all about?

BILLY: It's called "craziness"! It's runs rampant in this house.

NILANSA: You want to talk about "crazy"? Let's talk about this little Susie Smith.

LOUISA: I can't believe, William, that you've fallen for this trick yet again. I was so hoping this time would be different, for your sake, sweet boy.

BILLY: Her name is Susie Smith. I've known her for several years. For crying out loud, I've met her parents numerous times—had dinner at their house often the past three years. They only live an hour away.

RANDOLPH: John and Jane Smith, I suppose?

BILLY: *(shocked)* You know Susie's parents?

NILANSA: Tell me her parents' names are not John and Jane Smith!

BILLY: You all are making the wrong assumptions here! Susie is a sweet, normal girl from a small Alabama town. Her parents are simple people with simple names.

LOUISA: Very simple—and rather uncreative—names.

BILLY: Exactly! If someone were actually trying to pull off some kind of manipulative heist, do you think they would have set me up for three whole years ... using names like John and Jane ...

RANDOLPH: ... and Susie ... don't forget her.

BILLY: Oh, now you remember her name!

RANDOLPH: Well, before she was unremarkable, thus unrememberable. Now she's part of a major masterminded project designed to bring ruin to the Cavanaugh fortune.

BILLY: She is not a part of anything underhanded! She's an innocent ...

(Susie screams offstage and comes running in.)

SUSIE: Bentley Magnum Cavanaugh! I am not that kind of girl!

BILLY: *(alarmed)* What did he do?

SUSIE: What didn't he do!

(Bentley comes in buttoning up his shirt.)

BENTLEY: I was merely testing her memory. She said she had seen all my films, so I was re-enacting a scene from the movie ***The Trouble with Tigers***.

SUSIE: I don't recall any kitchen scene from that movie!

BENTLEY: Well, the scene didn't take place in a kitchen. I was just using my imagination.

MAID: *(running in desperately)* That pot is boiling over! I don't know what to do!

SUSIE: *(running out after the maid)* Oh, dear! Did it not occur to you to stir the thing? Use *your* imagination!

BENTLEY: *(following Susie out)* Exactly the point I was trying to make! Use your imagination!

BILLY: *(starting to run after Bentley)* Oh, no you don't

RANDOLPH: *(catching Billy by the arm)* Have we suddenly sparked a little concern in your mind?

NILANSA: Thinking sweet, little Susie might not be so sweet after all?

LOUISA: ... or perhaps that she might not even be this so-called "Susie".

BILLY: Would you all stop it? I'm not concerned *about* Susie—I'm concerned *for* her! Bentley was practically foaming at the mouth and she's *my* fiancé!

NILANSA: Then it would seem you have nothing to worry about. Surely Susie won't succumb to his unmatchable manly charms if she's so devoted to you.

(twins come in with candy again)

NILANSA: Are you girls eating candy again? That is not a part of your diet regimen.

TAMI-TINA: The maid gave it to us.

TINA-TAMI: She was gonna give us more, but then the kitchen caught on fire.

BILLY: What!

LOUISA: Oh, dear heavens! I thought you said the girl could cook, William!

TAMI-TINA: Oh, Susie can cook ...

TINA-TAMI: She's whipping up quite a spread in there.

TAMI-TINA: The maid caught it on fire.

RANDOLPH: Should I go to the study and call the fire department?

TINA-TAMI: Susie put it out.

RANDOLPH: She's putting out fires now, you say? I thought she was supposed to be a simple "narrator". Now we've got her acting as chef and fireman in the bowels of our kitchen. How do you explain that, William?

BILLY: She is *not* a narrator! She's a teller!

RANDOLPH: Teller, narrator—Sassy, Susie ... why is there so much dubious information where this girl is concerned?

LOUISA: We could hire a detective, you know—have him thoroughly check out her questionable past to find out exactly what she's been hiding.

NILANSA: I know a great one! He's the man that discovered my ex was cheating.

LOUISA: Wonderful! Take his name, Randolph, and let's get him started on the investigation right away.

BILLY: No! *(they look at him offended)* Susie is not this monster you're trying to make her out to be. In fact, right now she's in the kitchen trying desperately to hold onto her sanity by cooking a meal for all of you just to have something *normal* to do in the midst of all this craziness.

NILANSA: *(getting a fearful look, stands slowly and dramatically)* Oh ... my ... heavens!

LOUISA: What, dear?

NILANSA: She's going to poison us!

BILLY: What?!

RANDOLPH: For the love of Linus, why? Whatever have we done to deserve a massive murder like this?

BILLY: You have all lost your minds!

FANCY: *(jumping from the couch)* Armando! What if *she* killed Armando?

NILANSA: The picture is becoming quite clear now.

LOUISA: Oh, what a jumbled mess this all is! First, Armando is murdered, then Cooky quits, and now we're all about to eat ourselves to our deaths!

BILLY: She is no murderer!

GRANDMA KAT: *(comes running through screaming)* Tornado! Take cover! It's a tornado! *(runs out the other side of the stage)*

RANDOLPH: What in heaven's name is Mother doing now?

LOUISA: *(throwing her arms up)* Our whole household is falling apart!

FANCY: *(falling back to the couch wailing)* Armando!

MAID: *(comes in looking very disheveled)* Susie wants me to ask who prefers white meat or dark meat?

RANDOLPH: It's a trick! No! It's some kind of riddle!

LOUISA: We must figure it out! Maybe there's a chance we won't die!

BILLY: Ok, ok, ok! Enough! *(goes to call Susie)* Susie! Could you come out here a minute!

LOUISA: *(huddling next to Randolph)* I'm fearful. What will she do if she knows we're onto her plan?

NILANSA: We will be strong—we will face our end with dignity and confidence.

SUSIE: *(comes in followed by Bentley)* I hope this is important. I'm in the midst of brewing up something really special, and if I don't watch the pot it could turn out disastrous.

LOUISA: *(let's out a small scream)* Ahh!

SUSIE: Are you all right, Miss Louisa?

LOUISA: For the moment …

RANDOLPH: *(bravely)* What exactly did you mean by "do we prefer white meat or dark meat"?

SUSIE: *(slowly)* Do you prefer white meat or dark meat?

NILANSA: How sinister!

SUSIE: What? *(turns to maid)* What on earth did you ask them?

MAID: Just what you told me to ask. Look, I told all of you that cooking is not my area of expertise.

BILLY: *(trying to divert attention)* There's a good point—what exactly is your area of expertise?

TAMI-TINA: It's Armando, the pool guy.

MAID: *(slapping Tami's shoulder)* Hush your mouth, child!

FANCY: What?

TINA-TAMI: Yeah, we watch you sneak out of his bungalow every morning.

FANCY: What?

TAMI-TINA: And I don't think you were there just for the Pop-tarts.

TINA-TAMI: I don't blame you, though—for an old guy, he's hot.

FANCY: Tami-Tina! *(she gets the name wrong)* Don't talk about him that way!

TAMI-TINA: Hey! I'm Tami-Tina! She's Tina-Tami.

FANCY: Whatever! What kind of ridiculous names are those anyway?

NILANSA: *(offended)* They are the names given to them by a loving and caring mother who wants them in her life!

FANCY: Don't even start with me! *(back to the maid)* Explain to me, Miss ... Maid, exactly what was your relationship with Armando?

MAID: I don't have to answer that! Armando was a sweet, tender soul.

TINA-TAMI: And he was hot too.

FANCY: *(to Tina-Tami)* Stop it! You can't talk about him that way!

TINA-TAMI: The pool guy ... was ... hot.

NILANSA: Tina-Tami! Please tell me you did NOT have a fling with the pool guy!

FANCY: *(about to pass out)* Oh, dear heavens, no!

TAMI-TINA: Ewwwwww! You had a fling with Armando?

TINA-TAMI: No ... I just said he was hot.

FANCY: Stop it!

NILANSA: Would you please stop yelling at my daughter! She's done nothing wrong!

TINI-TAMI: *(in a sing-song fashion to taunt Fancy)* The pool guy is hot! The pool guy is hot!

FANCY: Don't talk about your father that way!

(Dead silence)

NILANSA: What did you say?

TAMI-TINA: Ewwwwww ... Mommy had a fling with the pool guy?

NILANSA: No! I thought about it ... but ... *(to Fancy)* You had a fling with the pool guy?

FANCY: His ... name ... is ... Armando!

TINA-TAMI: Armando is our father?

TAMI-TINA: Ewwwww! He is not!

TINA-TAMI: You said he was our father. *(Looks back and forth from Fancy to Nilansa ... then pulls out a handgun)* I want the truth, old ladies!

TAMI-TINA: Ahhh! She's got a gun!

NILANSA: Is that a prop, or did you buy it off the internet too?

TINA-TAMI: Does it matter? Just tell me the truth about Army!

MAID: Army? He told you to call him that too?

TINA-TAMI: Yeah. He and I were ... close.

FANCY and NILANSA: What?

FANCY: My stars and grasshoppers, have mercy on my soul!

TAMI-TINA: *(very subdued)* Ewwwww ...

FANCY: Tell me it's not so!

BENTLEY: It's a prop.

(Everyone looks at Bentley)

NILANSA: *(to Bentley)* What?

BENTLEY: You asked if it was a real gun or a prop. It's a prop. I can tell by the way ...

NILANSA, FANCY and TINA-TAMI: Shut up!

FANCY: *(to Tina-Tami)* Young lady, what exactly was the nature of your relationship with Armando?

TINA-TAMI: You're not my mother! I don't have to answer you!

FANCY: Yes, I am!

(Everyone now stares at Fancy)

TAMI-TINA: *(subdued to Fancy)* Mommy?

NILANSA: *(to Tami-Tina)* No, not you, dear. *(points to Tina-Tami)* Her.

RANDOLPH: What the blazes is going on here? Nilansa? Fancy?

FANCY: *(with a deep sigh)* When Bobby Bill and I split up, I found solace in the tender-hearted arms of Armando.

TAMI-TINA: *(subdued again)* Ewwwww ...

FANCY: When I discovered I was pregnant, I knew Nilansa was also. I was in no condition to raise a child.

NILANSA: I was on location with my husband's film in Africa.

LOUISA: Which husband might that be, dear?

NILANSA: Don't even start with me, woman.

FANCY: I told everyone I was doing a tour for charity in Asia. If it got out I was pregnant, you know Bobby Bill would have caused all kinds of trouble. I packed up and took off for Africa where I stayed with Nilansa until the babies were born.

RANDOLPH: Lands' sakes, girl! And they were both born on the same day?

NILANSA: They were actually five months apart.

TAMI-TINA: I knew it! *(pointing to Tina-Tami)* I knew I was older than you by more than just three minutes!

TINA-TAMI: Okay, *(trying to stay calm)* so let me get this all straight. The overly dramatic, over-the-hill actress is not my mother—but the boot-wearing country singer is? The wimpy actor in those lame safari movies is not my father—but the good-looking, and rather muscular pool guy is?

TAMI-TINA: Don't talk about my parents like that!

TINA-TAMI: *(to Tami-Tina)* And you! For fifteen years I have dressed like a fruitcake—hot pink and neon green lace! Ewwwwww!

TAMI-TINA: Well it certainly beats black!

TINA-TAMI: Don't even! *(she reaches and grabs her twin's blond wig off ... the entire room gasps)*

TAMI-TINA: Stop it! You'll ruin everything!

TINA-TAMI: *(pulls off her own wig and shakes out her hair)* Ruin? Ruin? I'm free! I'm not a blond! I'm not a twin! And I hate neon pink and green!

FANCY: Please tell me you did not have a fling with Armando!

TAMI-TINA: Ewwwwww!

TINA-TAMI: Of course not. He was always like a ... like a father to me. *(to Fancy)* Did he know?

(phone rings)

FANCY: I don't know. I told you he was a sensitive and perceptive soul. And now he's *(begins sobbing again)* gone!

(phone rings again)

TINA-TAMI: *(looks sadly at Fancy then embraces her)* Mom!

(phone rings again)

LOUISA: *(to the maid)* For crying out loud, girl, answer the phone!

MAID: *(moving to phone)* I really need to read over my job description again. Cooking? Answering phones? *(picks up phone)* Hello, Wisteria Mansion ... yes ... yes ... no ... no ... I understand. I will tell them. Goodbye. *(hangs up phone)* That was the police. *(sadly)* The autopsy report came back and the results are conclusive concerning Armando's death. *(everyone braces themselves for the news)* He was poisoned by an overdose of chlorine.

LOUISA: Ahhh! Poisoned?

FANCY: No! *(wails again as Tina-Tami comforts her)*

RANDOLPH: How on earth could such a thing happen? Where would someone get this ... chlorine poison?

BENTLEY: He works with the pool, Randolph. He would have a supply of chlorine around all the time.

(the maid leaves)

RANDOLPH: Is it at all possible that he did it to himself ... some sort of suicide?

LOUISA: Of course not! He wouldn't have deliberately poisoned himself and then gone for a swim in the pool! Someone *(gazes over to Susie)* obviously did it to him.

TINA-TAMI: But who? He was a good pool guy.

RANDOLPH: Well, what does this chlorine look like anyway? How can we find it?

TAMI-TINA: There's a box of it in the pool house. They look like little, white hockey pucks.

(During all of this exchange, Susie has found a chlorine tablet in the apron pocket and has been nervously playing with it for some time now.)

TAMI-TINA: *(pointing at Susie)* That's it! That's a chlorine tablet!

(everyone now stares at Susie)

SUSIE: What?

LOUISA: You really did it? You killed the pool guy?

SUSIE: What? No! I didn't even know the pool guy!

FANCY: How could you? *(begins wailing again)*

SUSIE: Are you kidding me? This isn't even my apron! *(she looks around for the maid)* The maid put it on me! Where is she?

(At this point Billy sits on the couch and puts his head in his hands in disbelief.)

NILANSA: We warned you, William! What kind of girl are you trying to bring into the family this time?

SUSIE: I did not kill the pool guy!

TINA-TAMI: Murderer! Murderer!

SUSIE: You people are crazy! If anybody is guilty of circumstantial evidence, it would be the maid! This is her apron!

RANDOLPH: *(walks to Susie with arms folded)* You ... are ... good. You seemed so sincere ... and so sweet.

SUSIE: I am sweet! I would never even think about killing anybody!

BENTLEY: Circumstantial evidence, you say? That's a mighty official word from someone claiming to be so innocent.

RANDOLPH: What possible motive could you have for wanting to kill the pool guy?

LOUISA: She must have known him before.

TINA-TAMI: *(waves her gun toward Susie)* That's it! You had some tawdry past with him, and when you saw him here you were afraid he would blow your sweet little innocent cover!

BENTLEY: Excellent deduction, child. There may be room for you yet in my next project.

TINA-TAMI: Really?

TAMI-TINA: Or … you knew the pool guy years before and came here specifically to murder him.

SUSIE: No!

BENTLEY: Wait … it's all making sense now. You've never had intentions of marrying poor William! You merely knew the gullible man would be the perfect way to ease yourself into Wisteria where you could off the unsuspecting pool guy!

LOUISA: What? You used my William? Not again!

RANDOLPH: How reprehensible!

SUSIE: No!

NILANSA: Well, I for one, am shocked and appalled.

TAMI-TINA: Me too, Mommy.

TINA-TAMI: Can't believe I'm actually saying this—but I agree with my … sister. You killed Army?

SUSIE: No!

FANCY: Exactly how well did you know him?

NILANSA: Yes, dear Susie Smith, if indeed that is your name, how exactly did you know the pool guy? What was the nature of your relationship?

SUSIE: *(exploding with overcome distraught emotion and screaming at the top of her lungs)* I love Billy Cavanaugh! I want to marry him! But I never want to step foot around you people again! I ... did ... not ... kill ... Edwardo!
    (everyone gets quiet and just stares)
FANCY: *(in a loud whisper)* Armando!
    *(Let the silence linger, then Randolph
    begins to clap and say, "Bravo!")*
RANDOLPH: I'll have to say that was rather marvelous, child.
LOUISA: You have managed to stand more than I imagined anyone could.
SUSIE: *(emotionally undone)* What are you talking about?
BILLY: *(getting up and going to Susie)* So the murder was staged?
RANDOLPH: But, of course.
SUSIE: What? You set all of this up ... you intentionally framed me to look like a murderer?
LOUISA: And though I can't believe I'm saying this—you came through with flying colors ... at last.
SUSIE: Why? *(deplete of energy)* Why on earth would you do this to a total stranger ... to someone coming into your house to meet your family for the first time?
RANDOLPH: Isn't it obvious? Do you know how many people try to worm their way into Wisteria ...
LOUISA: ... hoping for a glance or a chance meeting with a Cavanaugh? And poor William—he's been duped by more women than we can even begin to count.
RANDOLPH: The rest of us run in show business circles —we seldom meet ... regular people.
LOUISA: We had to make sure you weren't another parasitic girl latching onto our gullible William setting him up for yet another heartbreak. You do understand, don't you?

SUSIE: *(takes off apron slowly, folds it and hands to Louisa)* I don't honestly know what to say. All I know is that you are the most insane ... crazy ... lunatic bunch of people I have ever met. I told Billy I didn't even want to have children with him because I was scared to death to pass on this gene pool. *(to Billy)* I'll be frank with you—I don't think I can even bear to marry you anymore. You may be sweet, gentle and somewhat ... unremarkable ... compared to this bunch, but if this is the blood that flows through your veins, I would live in fearful expectation each day of you just going off the edge like the rest of them. *(takes off her ring, hands it to him, and turns to leave)* I'm sorry—I can't marry you.

LOUISA: Hold on, dear. *(takes Susie's arm to stop her from leaving)* As long as we're confessing secrets, I suppose it's time for me to let the biggest cat out of the bag.

RANDOLPH: Louisa! Are you certain you want to do this?

LOUISA: *(she nods)* It's time. *(she goes to Billy)* Dear boy, I had always hoped you would find your destiny here with us—that somehow you would find your own star to hang onto. But, alas ... that is not to be. *(motions toward Susie)* This dear girl is where your future belongs. *(she sighs)* There isn't a drop of Cavanaugh blood running through your body, my son.

(all are stunned and gasp)

BILLY: What?

SUSIE: I don't understand. I saw all the reruns of the year you were pregnant with him! I saw him as a baby and little boy on your show!

RANDOLPH: Prosthetics.

NILANSA: You've got to be kidding me.

FANCY: And we thought *we* had a big secret.

BENTLEY: You *did* have a big secret!

RANDOLPH: We had it all planned out. We wanted a child badly, but it wasn't to be.

LOUISA: We decided to adopt, but ... well ... wanted everyone to believe the child was our own.

RANDOLPH: It was great for publicity.

LOUISA: We wrote it into our scripts for the show.

RANDOLPH: Even did a lullaby album.

LOUISA: It jumpstarted our fleeting careers. *(to Billy)* So, you see, dear, as much as we hated to admit it, you really weren't like us ... aren't like us.

BILLY: *(looks stunned for a moment then suddenly jumps in the air and shouts)* Yahoo! I'm normal! I'm really normal! *(gets down on one knee and takes Susie's hand)* Susie, you are the best thing that's ever happened to me. Please don't leave me. I'll do anything to make you stay. If it means never coming back here again, then I'll do it. But don't walk away from me. Please. I love you, Susie, with all my heart.

(Susie looks around, reaches up to her face and faints. Bentley catches her.)

NILANSA: Impressive!

LOUISA: Wasn't it though? Exactly how did she do that? *(begins to imitate Susie's faint)* Catch me, will you, Randolph? *(faints identically)*

BLACKOUT

ACT TWO
Scene Two

SCENE: *Billy and Susie are sitting on the parlor couch alone, this time with Billy holding an open bottle of liquor, Susie holding a glass, and both having dazed looks.*

BILLY: Rough day ...
SUSIE: Very ...
BILLY: On the bright side, you didn't have to cook after all.
SUSIE: True ... nor am I a murderer.
BILLY: True. *(holds up the bottle to offer more)* Would you like some more?
SUSIE: Yeah, I think so. *(takes the whole bottle from him and turns it up)*
BILLY: Feeling better yet?
SUSIE: Who knows? They say alcohol dulls your senses.
BILLY: Have you ever had liquor before?
SUSIE: Only in cough syrup. *(sighs)* Until this day, the biggest need in my life was to merely squelch a cold. *(takes another drink)* But it could have been worse—there really could have been a murder, the evidence could have been legitimately planted on my person, and I could be sitting in a jail cell facing twenty years to life for first degree murder.
BILLY: My family wouldn't have let it happen. They would have bailed you out, hired a major lawyer, and gotten you off with a minor slap on the wrist.

SUSIE: Well, that's comforting. Where is the pool guy anyway? If he wasn't actually murdered, he's still ... up and at 'em, somewhere.

BILLY: Somewhere ...

(silence as they sigh a few moments)

BILLY: You do realize they're all highly impressed with you now?

SUSIE: *(she gives him an astonished stare)* Why? Because I fainted?

BILLY: Well, you did a lot more than faint ...

SUSIE: Yes, I ranted like a raving lunatic trying to declare my innocence.

BILLY: Yes, you did ... *(imitates his father's accent)* and what a splendid job you did, my dear. Ranting and raving—raving and ranting. It was quite a marvelous display! Either the dear girl is truly innocent, or she is a better actress than all of us put together! *(speaks normal again)* You know Mother and Nilansa spent all afternoon imitating your faint. They've gotten rather good at it.

SUSIE: I'm not sure if I should be honored or humiliated.

BILLY: Oh, honored for certain. They say imitation is the highest form of flattery.

(she does Linus salute)

BILLY: That wasn't a Linus quote—at least I don't think it was.

SUSIE: Oh ... should I take it back then? Will something bad happen to me if I salute Linus and he didn't really say it?

BILLY: Surely you've noticed that Linus gets credit for saying a lot of things he probably never said.

SUSIE: *(takes another drink)* Did you ever want to go into show business at all? Did the bug never bite you ... even a little bit? You were surrounded by all this ... talent ...

BILLY: ... drama ...

SUSIE: ... that too ... and yet it seems to have had no pull on you.

BILLY: Two great things have happened in my life, Susie. The first was when I finally mustered up enough courage to ask you if you needed any help on your taxes.

SUSIE: *(smiling)* And I thought you were sincerely wanting to help with those taxes.

BILLY: I sincerely wanted to do anything to be close enough to have a conversation with you.

SUSIE: And after that first meeting you asked me if I wanted to "crunch some numbers as we munched on lunch."

(Billy does Linus salute)

SUSIE: Linus said that? *(he nods—she takes another drink)* I guess we'll never completely escape your family.

LOUISA: *(offstage)* Yoo-hoo! Everyone decent?

BILLY: Mother! I told you before—of course we are!
(Randolph and Louisa enter with Louisa holding a gift bag)

LOUISA: Don't be offended, dear William. If you only knew how many times I've walked into this parlor over the years to find Bentley and ... oh, never mind. *(looks sweetly at them)* I have something special for you.

BILLY: I think we've had more than enough from the Cavanaughs, Mother.

LOUISA: I'm so sorry, dear. I suppose I should have told you years ago that you were adopted. It might have taken off some of the pressure you felt to try and conform to us.

BILLY: *(getting a bit angry)* I don't care about me! You can do whatever you want to me. It's how you treated Susie! She came here simply wanting to meet my family and you all framed her for murder!

SUSIE: Billy, stop—it's okay. They did it because they loved you and didn't want to see you duped again.

LOUISA: And we were very, very wrong to do so. It does my heart much good to see you've found someone who truly loves you for who you are. If I'm guilty of anything, it's from only wanting to protect my son.

BILLY: Yes, your ignorant, incapable, untalented, adopted son.

LOUISA: Oh, William, had I actually carried you and birthed you myself, I still couldn't love you anymore. No matter what you are, or what you think about me, you will always be the son of my heart.

RANDOLPH: Don't be angry with your mother. She truly does love you.

BILLY: Clearly, that's why she's tried to sabotage the only good thing that's ever happened to me.

SUSIE: It's okay, Billy. I'm okay.

BILLY: You're intoxicated. You're forgetting all that happened today.

SUSIE: Trust me—there's not enough liquor in the county to make me forget what happened today.

RANDOLPH: Sweet, Susie, you truly are a gem.

BILLY: It's a miracle! You still remember her name!

RANDOLPH: Yes, and I don't imagine I will ever forget it again. Susie—the lovely creature that managed to bring meaning and purpose to your tortured soul. *(to Louisa)* That would make a great movie. I must tell the writers about this.

BILLY: Tortured soul?! The only reason I was tortured was because I was an outcast in my own family! I was raised to believe I was somehow a genetic mutant in the midst of ...

SUSIE: *(stopping him)* Billy—it's all okay now. It's over. The truth is out, we're getting married, I know everything now—no secrets, and you are certainly not a genetic mutant. *(to the parents)* Ms. Louisa and Mr. Randolph, I still admire you and your work. You're both very talented, and you raised a wonderful son. I'll always be grateful to you for that.

LOUISA: I hope you understand why we did what we did.

SUSIE: I'll say that I can understand in your unusual ... and rather warped way, you were trying to protect your son.

LOUISA: But can you forgive us?

SUSIE: *(sighs)* You thought you were doing what was right. *(pause)* Of course, I can.

LOUISA: Dear, sweet, child! *(holds out gift)* And now, please take this gift and keep it always as a reminder of how much William and you mean to us.

SUSIE: *(takes gift)* Of course, I will.

(Susie takes bag but is interrupted when
Bentley, Nilansa and Fancy enter, quite tipsy from alcohol.
They notice everyone and try to stifle themselves.)

BENTLEY: Pardon us for intruding, but we wanted to check on Susie.

FANCY: Last time we saw you, you were laid out on the parlor floor.

LOUISA: Not now, not now—she's fine. She's about to open our gift.

(Nilansa and Fancy excitedly move to the
left and sit in the chairs, Bentley stands next to them.
Susie pulls out an Emmy award from the gift bag)

BILLY: You gave us one of your awards?

SUSIE: Not just any award. Look at the date.

BILLY: The year I was born?

RANDOLPH: That was the year we won the award for best television comedy.

LOUISA: Because I was pregnant with you ... well ... pretending to be ... it was written into all the scripts.

RANDOLPH: She hobbled and bobbled all over the set.

NILANSA: She hobbled and bobbled everywhere! You were even pregnant here at Wisteria.

LOUISA: Alas, I so longed to bear a child. *(sits next to Billy)* It was the role of a lifetime. I played the part for nine precious months—on and off the stage.

FANCY: I'll say. I'll have to hand it to you—you had us all convinced.

RANDOLPH: Yes, she did a marvelous job. So marvelous, in fact, that no one knew otherwise. And the public, the producers, the world—well, the truth is, the pregnancy revived our careers. Everyone followed young William from birth up through six years old when we decided to stop the show and go back to Broadway.

BENTLEY: *(to Billy)* You always were such an odd, little fellow. I can't believe it never crossed my mind that it all ... well ... was a show.

NILANSA: The woman walked around the world looking pregnant for nine months! She walked around the house looking pregnant for nine months! Why would anyone suspect otherwise? It doesn't get much crazier than that!

GRANDMA KAT: *(off stage)* I'll get you, my little pretties! *(twins come running in followed by Grandma Kat)*

TAMI-TINA: Make her stop!

TINA-TAMI: This is one crazy family!

(Maid comes in and grabs Grandma Kat)

MAID: Dorothy! Wait!

GRANDMA KAT: Ahhhh! Flying monkeys! *(runs out with maid following her)*

NILANSA: I stand corrected.

SUSIE: *(going to Louisa)* I thank you both for this gift. It will be front and center in our home. And thank you for raising Billy to be such a wonderful man. He may not be your son by blood *(Billy raises his head and mouths a "thank you" toward heaven)*, but he is still your son. He wouldn't be who he is today had some other couple adopted him. Thank-you. *(she hugs them both)*

(Armando enters)

ARMANDO: Excuse me? I hope I am not interrupting anything important.

EVERYONE: Armando!

SUSIE: The pool guy?

ARMANDO: That would be me, yes.

SUSIE: You look so ... alive.

ARMANDO: Thank you. Yes, it was hard to hold my breath for so long as I lay face down in the pool waiting to be pulled out.

FANCY: *(stands up next to him)* Hello again, Armando.

TINA-TAMI: You know what? I think it's time we had our own little family meeting.

FANCY: I think you're right.

ARMANDO: I do not understand.

TAMI-TINA: Boy, are you in for a big surprise.

ARMANDO: But first, I wanted to inform everyone that the pool is now ready.

RANDOLPH: Yes, thank-you, Armando.

ARMANDO: Not at all. *(Fancy and Tina-Tami loop their arms in his)* I do not know what we are doing, but so far I like it very much?

(the trio exits)

BILLY: Now, if everyone wouldn't mind, Susie and I have an early flight back tomorrow. It's been a long, exhausting, nerve-racking day, and it's late.

LOUISA: Of course. We understand dear. We'll see you both off in the morning.

(They all say "goodbyes" and everyone exits except Billy and Susie.)

SUSIE: You never finished telling me about the two greatest things that have ever happened to you. You said the first was mustering up the courage to talk with me. What was the second?

BILLY: The second was learning today that I was actually adopted.

SUSIE: *(she looks at him in surprise)* Really? It ranks that high?

BILLY: Imagine growing up in this and thinking that "this" is normal. Then leaving this and realizing it's not normal at all, but everyone you're related to thinks it is normal. *(he looks at her and smiles big)* Do you realize what this means?

SUSIE: I have no idea.

BILLY: *(he stands)* It means I'm normal! I'm really, really normal. I'm not a talentless, genetic mess-up of the Cavanaughs. I'm a normal transplant that was grafted into their vine ... only I kept my own DNA. I'm normal!

SUSIE: Thank goodness.

(Grandma Kat comes running in with a guitar case)

GRANDMA KAT: *(to Susie)* Are you a good witch or a bad witch?

BILLY: Grandma! Susie is not a witch!

SUSIE: *(stands)* It's okay. I think I can handle this. *(to Grandma)* I'm a good witch.

GRANDMA: I knew it! *(puts down her guitar case and hugs Susie)* There's no place like home. *(picks up guitar case to leave)*

BILLY: Grandma Kat? Are you playing guitar now?

GRANDMA KAT: But of course! I'm going to be a governess for the Captain. I must be off! The hills are alive, you know! *(she exits)*

BILLY: I'm not related to her, you know.

SUSIE: *(nodding her head)* Actually ... you are.

BILLY: No! I just explained ...

SUSIE: *(she stops him with a kiss)* Whether you like it or not, this indeed is your family. DNA doesn't matter. Who you are—the wonderful man that you are—is because of them. All the tributaries of the Cavanaughs have flowed into you through the years. Just because you didn't follow in their footsteps doesn't mean they didn't influence you. Being the only normal person in a family like this would have destroyed some people. *(kisses him again)* But it made you the strong gentle giant that you are today. Fate placed you here, and I will love your family for who they all are simply because I love you ... William Desmond Cavanaugh.

BLACKOUT

DAPHNE C. MURRELL

For more information or other writings from the author,
visit www.daphnemurrell.com.

www.ingramcontent.com/pod-product-compliance
Lightning Source LLC
Chambersburg PA
CBHW071319040426
42444CB00009B/2049